True Crime Online

Shocking Stories of Scamming, Stalking, Murder, and Mayhem

J. A. Hitchcock

CyberAge Books
Information Today, Inc.
Medford, New Jersey

First Printing, 2013

True Crime Online: Shocking Stories of Scamming, Stalking, Murder, and Mayhem

 Published by CyberAge Books, an imprint of Information Today, Inc., 143 Old Marlton Pike, Medford, New Jersey 08055.

While this book includes true stories, some names and details have been intentionally omitted to respect the wishes of certain individuals.

Library of Congress Cataloging-in-Publication Data

Hitchcock, Jayne A.
True crime online : shocking stories of scamming, stalking, murder, and mayhem / by J.A. Hitchcock.
p. cm.
Includes index.
ISBN 978-1-937290-00-9
1. Computer crimes--Case studies. 2. Cyberstalking--Case studies. 3. Online sexual predators--Case studies. 4. Murder--Case studies. I. Title.
HV6773.H576 2012
364.16'8--dc23
2012038252

Printed and bound in the United States of America

President and CEO: Thomas H. Hogan, Sr.
Editor-in-Chief and Publisher: John B. Bryans
VP Graphics and Production: M. Heide Dengler
Project Editor: Barbara Brynko
Cover Designer: Lisa Conroy

www.infotoday.com

For my husband, Chris,
who taught me how to love, laugh, and live again

Contents

Acknowledgments

Many thanks to the Portsmouth (New Hampshire) Police Department, especially retired Chief Lou Ferland, Police Chief Steve Dubois, and Sgt. Tom Grella. I signed up for their Citizen Police Academy and ended up learning so much about how law enforcement works, including fingerprinting, how mug shots are taken, the booking process, specialty teams like the K-9 units and local SWAT (called SERT), and beer "goggles." I also attended various demonstrations and made many new friends. We visited other police departments in the area and even paid a visit to the Rockingham County Jail, which reinforced in me to never, ever commit a crime. Lou, Steve, and Tom's patience with my seemingly endless questions for this book will never be forgotten!

Thanks to Jim Christy of the Department of Defense Cyber Crime Center for his help. I had to get a mug shot in person in Maryland, and he didn't hesitate to do that for me.

Thank yous go out to all of the police departments and people who allowed me to use their stories and photos for this book. I couldn't have done it without any of you!

A shout out to fellow writers Kate Flora and Margaret Press, who pointed me in the right direction when it came to getting all of the mug shots I needed.

Thank you to my editor, Barbara Brynko, for keeping me sane.

And a final thank you to my husband, Chris, who knew if he saw me typing madly to leave me alone, even if it meant that dinner would be late. He was my shoulder to cry on when I got frustrated, and he gamely listened to me when I told him about an interesting story I found online (at least I thought it was interesting). I married the best man ever!

About the Website

www.truecrime-online.com

For updates about the cases featured in this book and other information, visit the book's website at www.truecrime-online.com.

To follow or participate in the discussion of the book on Twitter, follow the hashtag *#netcrimes*. Also connect with the book on Facebook (www.facebook.com/truecrimeonline).

Please feel free to share your own stories and comments with the author at netcrimes@netcrimes.net.

Disclaimer

Neither the publisher nor the author makes any claim as to the results that may be obtained through the use of this website or of any of the internet resources it references or links to. Neither publisher nor author will be held liable for any results, or lack thereof, obtained by the use of this page or any of its links; for any third-party charges; or for any hardware, software, or other problems that may occur as the result of using it. The website is subject to change or discontinuation without notice at the discretion of the publisher and author.

Foreword

I met Jayne Hitchcock over a decade ago while I was filming a TV pilot called *Predators*. It showcased several victims of online and offline crime, primarily those who were being stalked. Jayne was asked to participate because of her expertise and knowledge of the internet as well as her involvement with related legislation.

Stalking can be a terrifying experience for victims. It is a crime of power and control. The most common forms of stalking in the physical world involve excessive phone calls, following the victim in person, leaving presents or notes on the victim's vehicle or at his or her home, sending letters via postal mail, making unexpected visits at the victim's home or workplace, sending text messages, and actual surveillance. Often, stalking is an attempt to force a relationship with someone who is unwilling to have a relationship, whether or not there was any type of involvement beforehand.

Cyberstalking is a newer form of the same crime and is occurring more often in our society because of the advent of the internet. With cyberstalking, a person is followed and pursued online via email, blogs, social networking sites, instant messaging, message boards, webcams, chat rooms, and more. You name the medium and a cyberstalker has probably found a way to use it to pursue a victim. A victim's privacy is invaded in what has become a 24-hour world. Not only can victims be stalked in person, they can be stalked online and via their cell phones, leaving them no chance to breathe or escape from the madness. Every movement can be watched. This type of harassment can disrupt the victims' lives and leave them feeling extremely fearful and threatened. Many feel they have nowhere to turn for help.

Cyberstalking and online harassment generally involve men stalking women, and in other cases, adult predators or pedophiles targeting innocent children. With the internet, predators don't need to leave their homes anymore to find or harass their targets. They have no fear of physical violence, since they believe that they cannot be physically touched in cyberspace.

The stories in this book are both frightening and real and depict things that can and do happen every day. They show us what can happen to people just like you and me, people who never thought they could become victims of online crimes.

Parents need to be aware of their children's online activities to protect them from pedophiles and predators. We must also remind children that if they are being bullied or manipulated online, they should log off or block the person immediately or just ignore them altogether. They should also feel comfortable enough to confide in a parent or a trusted adult if someone is scaring them online.

The same holds true for adults; we need to remember that the online world has plenty of bad guys in it just as the real world does. We cannot ignore the vast online world, which can be very frightening at times. When the internet became more accessible to the general public in 1993, there were only 5,000 websites. As of March 2012, that figure has grown to more than 640 million, according to Netcraft.

I encourage everyone to learn what happens on the internet, good and bad, so we can teach our children how to be safe and smart online and keep ourselves safe too.

An online stranger may entice you or your child into a conversation by pretending to be a friend. We may not know who the person communicating with us really is, but we tend to trust too much. We want to believe that people have our best interests at heart, but unfortunately, this isn't always the case, as you will read in the chapters that follow.

Because online crimes are real, the consequences can be life-transforming and even fatal. The emotional scars that result can persist long after the crime ends and can run the gamut from depression and anxiety to shame and loss of self-esteem. It's not only the victims who feel a sense of hopelessness and vulnerability, but their families and friends as well.

When I was a child, I was one of six girls who used to run around the neighborhood from house to house. Neither our parents nor any of us felt threatened. Life wasn't scary back then, and home was our safe haven. Today, our homes are not what they used to be. We must not let our privacy become permeated by evil. Let's put an end to these heinous crimes. Let's make our homes and communities safe again, online and offline.

Jayne, thank you for continuing to educate us and for doing everything to keep us safe.

Denise Brown
Advocate Against Violence
www.denisebrown.com

Introduction

The world has changed drastically over the past decade. The internet has played a huge part in that change, making the world more accessible to anyone of any age, race, or gender, wherever they live. From entertainment to education and from shopping to dating, the internet has provided an entirely new virtual world for everyone to enjoy. But it has also opened the door to criminals.

The internet is a breeding ground for murderers, kidnappers, child predators, scam artists, terrorists, hackers, and other criminals. In fact, the Federal Bureau of Investigation (FBI) Internet Crime Complaint Center found that in 2011 a record-setting 314,246 fraud complaints were filed, a 3.4 percent increase from 2010, with a monetary loss for victims at a staggering estimate of $485.3 million, almost double from the previous year. The complaints filed included FBI-related scams as the No. 1 complaint, followed by identity theft, advance fee scams, nondelivery of merchandise and/or payment, overpayment of services, work-from-home scams, FBI impersonation scams, and loan intimidation scams.

Psychologists have argued for years about what makes a criminal tick. Why do criminals scam people? Why do criminals kill people? Why do they threaten, abuse, rape? The list goes on and on.

Some blame it on a bad childhood or a mental illness; others claim it's the environment they grew up in. But it all comes down to this: No one can explain why some people become criminals, especially those who have absolutely no criminal past, no bad childhood, and no bad environment. Something inside of them just seems to snap.

The same applies to criminals on the internet, although some distinctions can be made.

There are scam artists who are out to get as much money as they can, who disappear and then reappear under another persona. This happens most often with online auctions, websites that offer free ads to sell items, spam (junk email) that have unbelievable products or services for sale, and the Nigerians who claim they have tons of money they want to share with you.

Then there are the people who have had relationships go sour and decide to take it out on another person online. This group includes not only ex-spouses and significant others, but family members, co-workers, fellow students, next-door neighbors, roommates—just about anyone who had a prior relationship with the victim.

Next are the cyberstalkers, who are much the same as offline stalkers: They are obsessed with their victims. You don't have to be a celebrity to have a stalker anymore.

Then there are the organized cybercriminals, the ones who know the ins and outs of the internet and can wreak havoc on individuals, take down websites, infiltrate government computers, plant viruses, and create Trojans, causing unspeakable online torment.

The last group of cyberstalkers can only be defined as perpetrators of Internet Road Rage. On real highways, people sometimes become so angry at other drivers that they chase them and often end up causing an accident. What makes them do it? What is the trigger that makes them lose all self-control? The same thing happens on the information superhighway. These stranger-on-stranger cases can be as mundane as someone not liking another person's username in a chat room, or getting upset because someone insulted an actor they like, or another perceived injustice. The cyberstalker taunts the user, gets a defensive reaction from the now-victim, which is perfectly normal, and then the harassment escalates. According to Working to Halt Online Abuse (WHOA), more than 30 percent of its cyberstalking cases in 2011 escalated to offline stalking.

You name it, it's happened online, and if it hasn't, chances are it will. Any part of the internet can be used against you. Just when you think you've seen it all, you'll read or hear about a new incident that happened on the internet.

The chapters in this book cover just some of these incidents. A cyberstalker focuses his attention on an unlucky victim, one who does not even know it, in Chapter 1, "What Amy Boyer Didn't Know Killed Her." Love gone wrong online is detailed in Chapter 2, "Deadly Love Triangle," followed by the story of an adulterer who sweet talks a woman (Chapter 3, "Don't Preach to Me") and another love story that turns into a nightmare for one woman (Chapter 4, "When Online Dating Victims Fight Back").

A young woman is stalked online and offline by someone claiming to "love" her in Chapter 5, "Just Trying to Help a Friend," and a famous ghost hunter becomes the target of a frenzied fan in Chapter 6, "Stalking Ghosts." Two international stings are covered, one that nets child pornographers (Chapter 7, "How to Catch 700 Online Sexual Predators") and another that catches online cannibals (Chapter 8, "Guess Who's For Dinner?"). See who was "The First Internet Serial Killer" in Chapter 9. Read the story of woman targeted by a stalker across the ocean in Chapter 10, "Swedish Phishing," and about when cyberbullies attack in Chapter 11, "Virtually Bullied to Death."

Online videos cause chaos in Chapter 12, "YouTube as Witness," and we learn how law enforcement uses the internet to catch criminals in Chapter 13, "They'll Be Watching You ... Online." Chapter 14, "The Killer Inside," delves into people who find a thrill in encouraging others to kill themselves. See how the internet wreaks havoc on the lives of several people in Chapter 15, "When Revenge and Hatred Are Fueled Online," and finally, learn how online ads can turn deadly in Chapter 16, "Craigslist Killers."

So why do online criminals do what they do? There is no simple answer. For those people who have a criminal history, as with most scam artists, the internet is just a new medium to ply their craft. As technology changes, so do the tactics of these criminals.

Often, online criminals adapt to newer technology much more quickly than law enforcement does, which is an advantage for the criminals and a disadvantage for their victims.

Statistics show that the majority of online criminals are white-collar, do not have a criminal record, and are considered normal, everyday people. They're married, single, divorced, or living with a significant other. They could be a lawyer, teacher, office worker, waiter, nurse, housewife, grandfather, or the kid who mows your lawn. They may be someone you never imagined could harm another person, online or off. Their neighbors usually only have good things to say about them.

I like to call this the Dr. Jekyll and Mr. Hyde syndrome. During the day, these people interact with others normally; then they go home, go online, and either have a target in mind to harass, stalk, or threaten, or they get involved in an Internet Road Rage situation.

In the old days, it would take more effort to commit a crime. You would have to actually go to a town hall or county office to get information about someone, and more often than not, you would have to pay for that information.

Today, the internet makes it so much easier to do the same thing, whether the victim is next door or in another country, and most of the time, the information is free. Once the campaign is launched against a victim, the majority of cybercriminals think they can keep their anonymity by using a free email account (such as Hotmail, Gmail, or Yahoo!) or a remailer (an online service that lets you send email messages through its website instead of through your email program), or by changing the From line in a message to an email address that doesn't exist. But they are wrong.

It always amazes me that some people who are supposed to be mature, responsible adults lose all sense of their morals, ethics, and manners online. It's as though they regress to grade school when bullies ruled the schoolyard. They appear to take great joy in making their victims miserable, until they get caught. When they know they can't get away with harassment and stalking, their first reaction is usually either, "I never meant to hurt anyone" or "I didn't mean for it to go that far." But remember: That's their reaction *after* they get caught.

I played a personal role in several of the stories in this book. As president of WHOA, I worked directly with some of the victims and was able to help them resolve situations before they escalated.

The good news is that almost all 50 U.S. states as well as many countries now have cyberstalking/harassment laws on the books. Many are also passing laws against cyberbullying, spam, and other online crimes. The bad news is that not all victims know there is help available to them if they are scammed, threatened, stalked, bullied, or harassed online.

If you don't believe me, read the real-life stories in this book about people who have been stalked, harassed, threatened, abused, bullied, scammed, and sometimes killed—all using the internet. These people are or were just like you and me. So don't ever say, "This will never happen to me," because it just might.

1

What Amy Boyer Didn't Know Killed Her

When the phone rang, Helen Remsburg picked up the receiver and answered with her usual cheery "Hello!"

The voice on the other end sounded desperate. "You have to come! It's Amy."

It took a few seconds for Helen to recognize the voice. It was John Bednar, her daughter's boss.

"Helen, please come. Amy. Amy. Oh my God. Hurry, Helen!"

Helen hung up the phone and quickly called her husband, Tim Remsburg, who worked close by to Bednar's orthodontics practice. Hearing the panic in his wife's voice, Tim ran to his car, jumped in, and headed to Bednar's office. On the way, he heard sirens and saw the flashing lights of several police cars and an ambulance barreling down the street toward him. Instinctively, he made a U-turn and followed the caravan, which stopped at the emergency entrance to the hospital.

Tim parked and ran into the hospital, but security ushered him into a waiting room where he sat alone for what seemed like a lifetime. A nurse finally came in and asked him whether his stepdaughter wore toe rings. Sure she did, he said, and asked when he could see Amy.

The nurse paused for a moment. "I'm sorry, Mr. Remsburg. Amy is dead."

Tim fell to his knees; he couldn't breathe. He staggered to the emergency room entrance as Helen drove up. She opened the car door and looked at Tim. She knew immediately that her daughter was dead.

Helen and Tim found the police in the emergency room and wanted answers. The police shared the details they knew: Amy Boyer had been shot by Liam Youens, a young man about their daughter's age. Apparently, Youens had pulled up to Amy's car in the parking lot near Bednar's office, called out her name, then shot her several times in the face and arms with a Glock 9mm semiautomatic before turning the gun on himself. Youens was pronounced dead at the scene.

Helen and Tim had never heard their daughter mention Youens, although both of them had attended Nashua High School at the same time in Nashua, New Hampshire, a few years earlier. When the Nashua police went to visit Youens's parents that night, they found a connection of sorts between the two. They confiscated Youens's computer and discovered two online diaries, on Tripod.com and GeoCities.com, dating back at least 2 years. The police began to cobble together a tale of obsession and murder.

Youens first saw Amy during a church youth group meeting when they were both in eighth grade. He wrote in his online journal that he simply "fell in love" with Amy but watched her from afar, never letting her know how he felt. By the 10th grade, he waited until she passed him in the hall and just stood and stared. His was a growing obsession, as the following excerpts from his websites make clear.

> Whenever I was around Amy, I knew she was thinking of me. She would act as though she didn't notice me, whether or not I was staring at her (I actually didn't do it all the time, much less later in the year). To pretend that you don't notice someone uses twice as much concentration on that person than if you just ignored them. She even went as far as to brush by me in the lunch room, I even tried to avoid it, but she would have none of that. A normal person would have kept right, but because, "She had no idea I was there (yah-right)" she stayed in the center of the hall.

On one of his websites, Youens later wrote:

> Oh great, now I'm really depressed, hmmm ... looks like it's suicide for me. Car accident? Wrists? A few days later I think, "hey, why don't I kill her too?" was the basic plan for the next half decade, I work fast don't I?

On December 12, 1997, Youens wrote the following post on the alt.suicide.holiday discussion group about slitting his wrists:

> The best way to do it is this: - get a very large bowl, full of ice water ... lots of ice - put your arm in it for an hour (hurts at first) - get a razor or sharp knife, exactor knife good - cut along the wrist where it meets the hand - then cut 45 degrees down across your wrist - then down center along your arm until it starts to hurt - note: when I tried this, right before I cut. I dropped the knife and vomited.

Youens wrote online about his frustrations, his dreams, his anger, and his obsession for Amy, and then stalked her in real life. He borrowed his mother's car several times, drove it to Amy's house, and parked across the street. He would park for hours near her house, smoking, thinking, and dreaming. He lived to see her just one more time, and his paranoia escalated. One day as he waited near Amy's house, a police car drove past him. He later wrote on his website that he was sure the police were "onto him." Youens was convinced that Amy's stepfather also "knew" about his obsession with Amy. But he had a plan: He was going to kill Amy.

His collection of firearms grew, too, including an AR-15 and a Glock. He took photos of himself posing with the guns and posted them on his websites, noting the purchase price and even musing about murdering Amy in the following excerpt:

> Murder: Subplan: NHS (Nashua High School). I'm trying to remember when lunch starts, 10:05 I think, I believe 10:20 would be a good time for the attack. I plan to start shooting people in the courtyard as fast as I can. Reload, I am told that two Nashua Police officers will be in the school (this is why I need a vest). If those cops don't

> blow my brains out, I figure I'll have one minute before the cavalry comes ... ill go for head shots head shots head shots! They are a MUST.

Amy wasn't Youens's only target. The young man also flagged fellow Nashua High student Owen Banks. Youens wrote online that he once drove to Banks's house and saw him taking out the trash. He claimed that their eyes locked as they stared at each other, but Banks would later testify that he didn't remember the incident. In fact, he didn't even know Youens.

For the most part, the internet was a safe place in 1999; you could surf, plan a vacation, chat with new friends from around the world, go shopping, play games, and have fun. Helen and Tim never thought to enter their daughter's name into a search engine to check on any personal information about her that appeared. Had they done so, Youens's obsession with Amy might well have been discovered:

> Where I am noone will see me
> People only can when they are far
> Curled u in myself is where I belong
> The pain leaves me empty waiting to die
> It's hard to go I fear I never will
> Scared to live scared to die
> Seventy years of misery is my fate
> Can anyone have the answer?
>
> —Liam Youens, undated

Youens posted, "If I had a life myself, I really wouldn't care even if I was in love with her. I don't love her anymore, I wish I did but I don't. I wish I could have killed her in High school. I need to kill her so I can transport myself back into high school."

He wanted to set his plan in motion and find a place to kill Amy. He began searching online for her workplace, trying various investigative websites without any luck. Then, in early September 1999, he found Docusearch.com, which claimed it would provide a workplace address for anyone. But first he needed her Social Security number, which he also requested from Docusearch.com. Within days, he had the number and submitted the request for her workplace address. In all, he paid less than $150 for the information.

"It's actually obscene what you can find out about people on the internet," Youens posted. "I imagined what it would be like to know where she worked, a wonderful feeling a 'non-reality' thing like having a gun in algebra class to shoot her. Docusearch pulled through like a dream."

Tripod.com and GeoCities.com—the websites that hosted Youens's online diaries—claimed that his pages drew little traffic, but there is no way to substantiate this. When Youens's posts were removed less than 24 hours following the murder/suicide, a message in a guestbook on one of his pages read, "Nice page. Very informative. Keep it up." The police also found a series of emails between Youens and someone named Pieter from Greece who was apparently goading the young man into killing Amy. But that wasn't all.

"Pieter recommends I go on a rampage, but I don't know," Youens wrote. "I think [Amy] may be taking the whole 'I love life' thing bit too far. Now she's finally happy, but she could have been happy with a good career." And later, "Maybe she really will be a dentist. … Oh shit."

Youens staked out Bednar's office during September 1999 and kept track of Amy's schedule: when she arrived, when she left, how long she was gone, where she parked, and her route to and from work.

On one of his pages, he wrote:

> In the last 4 years I have had 3 or 4 dreams about Amy, but in the last month I've dreamt about her every single night. The last dream I had Amy was pregnant, so I stabbed the fetus through her, then cut her throat down to the bone, and broke her neck with my hand. She is either at Bednar's and not at home or at home and not at Bednar's. When she gets in [to work] I'll drive up to her car blocking her in, window to window I'll shoot her with my glock. On October 7 [1999] I was making excuses because I was scared. I still feel uncomfortable about sitting in the parking lot. I pray to God that [she] parks on the street like last friday, but I doubt it. My mother is going on vacation so I would be able to use her car. That may make me bold enough to park in the lot at 4:30.

On October 12, 1999, he wrote: "I saw her car on the street the perfect place. I parked my car there and sat at 4:35, but by 5:05 she still wasn't there, what a waste of a perfect opportunity. I drove around and saw that she left around 5:45, but I didn't see her and had no place to shoot. I would have done it. I feel good now."

The Nashua Police Department's 489-page report on the case noted that 15 minutes before the murder/suicide on October 15, 1999, Youens posted a final message on his webpages: "Pieter see if I did it." Then he placed a link to the local television station site, WMUR-TV.

On that day, as Youens sat in his mother's car, he watched Amy leave Bednar's office with two co-workers. The trio walked through the parking lot, chatting and laughing. As Amy waved goodbye, she opened her car door and slid into the driver's seat. She put her purse on the passenger seat and started the engine. As another car pulled up to hers, she heard someone call her name. She looked over to see Youens and a gun pointed at her head.

Instinctively, Amy covered her face with her arms, but it did nothing to protect her from the 8–10 rounds that struck her face and arms. The gunshots stopped for a few seconds; then one final shot rang out as Youens put the Glock in his mouth and pulled the trigger.

When the gunshots ended, a series of frantic 911 calls began. Then, it was Bednar's call to Helen and her call to her husband, and life as they knew it had changed forever.

A few months after Amy's death, her mother and stepfather launched a public campaign to spread the word about online safety, encouraging internet users to conduct a search regularly on their names and learn safe surfing practices. They appeared on talk shows, were featured on the nightly news, and testified before Congress, always promoting awareness of the potential dangers that lurked online.

On March 11, 2004, Helen reportedly received an $85,000 settlement from a lawsuit she waged against Docusearch.com. After 4 long years, Amy's family finally felt that a level of justice had been served. The settlement wouldn't bring Amy back, but it generated publicity and fueled greater public awareness about the way private information is bought and sold on the internet.

"We want other people to do what we didn't know how to do back then," Helen said. "Put your name, your children's names in a search engine and see what might be out there."

Left: Amy Boyer, stalked unknowingly and then murdered by Liam Youens
Above: One of the many guns Youens owned [Photos courtesy of Tim Remsburg]

Youens's website [Courtesy of Tim Remsburg]

2

Deadly Love Triangle

"If I were to plead guilty to this, could I get the death penalty?" asked 47-year-old Thomas Montgomery. He waited for the police officer to respond.

Erie County sheriff's deputy Gregory McCarthy paused for a moment before asking Montgomery if he understood his Miranda rights, but Montgomery didn't respond. After being escorted back to the interview room and left to think about it, Montgomery didn't sit alone for long before he quickly admitted that he understood his rights.

Montgomery had come to the sheriff's office that morning of his own free will and signed a statement acknowledging his involvement in a murder that had shocked Buffalo, New York, less than 2 weeks earlier. Convinced that they had their man, the police were taking pains to build an air-tight case. With mounds of evidence to wade through before they could issue an arrest warrant—including three computers they had confiscated, one from Montgomery's home—investigators released Montgomery on his own recognizance. (Perhaps surprisingly, the police had to let Montgomery go, even with a signed confession, until they could dig up enough evidence to issue an arrest warrant.)

The story was a chilling one. On September 15, 2006, 22-year-old Brian Barrett had clocked out at 10 PM after finishing his shift at Dynabrade Corp., a power tool plant just outside Buffalo. He climbed into the cab of his white pickup and put his key in the ignition.

Suddenly, three bullets tore through the driver's side window, killing him almost instantly. Brian never saw it coming.

The young man's body remained in the truck until Monday morning, when a co-worker saw the vehicle in the parking lot and went to investigate. The co-worker called the police, and investigators descended on the Dynabrade parking lot en masse to seal the crime scene and begin interviewing Brian's co-workers. An officer was dispatched to nearby Lockport with the sad task of notifying Deb and Dan Barrett that their son had been murdered.

As police began questioning Dynabrade employees, the tale of an online love triangle began to unfold. Police learned that Brian and Montgomery had been co-workers and friends before developing an online relationship with the same woman, whom they knew as "Jessi."

It had all started in the spring of 2005, when an 18-year-old Marine named "Tommy" began chatting online with 17-year-old Jessi from West Virginia. They were both frequenting a website called Pogo.com, where users can play games online and interact with other people via Club Pogo. Tommy began to confide in Jessi, telling her that his mother had died of cancer. Then he shared one of his most intimate secrets: He had raped a cheerleader in high school and turned himself in to police. Jessi was sympathetic. Later, he told her that he had joined the Marine Corps because his dad had been a Marine, and that he was going to be deployed to Iraq.

As time went on, Tommy and Jessi stepped up their communications, chatting not only on Pogo.com but through Myspace and Yahoo! Messenger. They spoke on the phone for about 10 minutes each day before and after Tommy's alleged military duties. When Tommy was suddenly deployed to Iraq, his father appeared online to forward correspondence and photos between Jessi and Tommy.

At one point, Tommy became possessive of Jessi, accusing her of sending photos of herself to other men online and cheating on him, though they had never met in person. Denying the allegations, Jessi mailed Tommy a pair of her thong underwear, along with a silver heart necklace ("The key to my heart," she called it) as a token of her love for him. Tommy accepted the gifts and her pledge of love, but his father allegedly sent a threatening email, warning her not to hurt his son. On Christmas Day 2005, Tommy proposed marriage and Jessi accepted, although the couple had yet to meet face-to-face.

During the police investigation that followed Brian's murder and the confession of Montgomery, the truth emerged that the online personas of both young Tommy and his father were played by just one man—Montgomery himself. Jessi turned out to be 50-year-old Mary Shieler, who had used her daughter's first name and photographs to get to know Tommy online.

As the online romance developed, overweight, middle-aged Montgomery began telling his co-workers that he was going to leave his wife and move to West Virginia where Jessi, his true love, was waiting for him. In his fantasy world, Montgomery imagined he could get into shape to become the guy Jessi would accept in spite of their supposed age difference.

But Montgomery's real-life wife, Cindy, suspected something was going on. Her husband was spending far too much time online late at night and wouldn't let his teenage daughters use the computer at all. It was clear that he was trying to hide something. Cindy discovered a package Jessi had mailed to her husband and realized he was involved in an online relationship, apparently with a teenage girl. She wrote a letter to Jessi, enclosing a snapshot of the real Montgomery.

"From what I am pulling from your letters you are much closer to [my daughter's] age than mine let alone Tom's," Cindy wrote. "Are you over the age of 18? In this alone, he can be prosecuted as a child predator." She added, "As you can see, Tom's not 18. He's married and he's a father of two. He's 47 and I'm his wife. You've obviously been fooled."

With that, Cindy confronted Montgomery with her discovery about his secret online life and told him she wanted a divorce. He didn't argue; he simply moved into the basement.

After Jessi received Cindy's letter, reality set in, and she began her search for a new, younger man. She started by looking at Tommy's list of friends on Pogo.com. She remembered Tommy mentioning a friend named Brian and contacted him after finding his profile under

"Beefcake1572." She confided in Brian about her involvement with the older man, and Brian confirmed Montgomery's age, marital status, and the rest. She asked Brian if he was really 22, explaining that she didn't want to get tricked again into falling in love with a much older man. Brian assured her that he actually was 22, and the two started an online relationship, playing Lottso (a game similar to bingo) on Pogo.com. Before long, they weren't just playing Lottso; they were engaging in cybersex.

While Jessi toyed with Brian's affections, she continued to email Montgomery, even though she now knew the truth about him. She taunted him with the news that she was getting to know Brian online, and Brian began bragging about the relationship at work, which infuriated Montgomery. The trio began exchanging messages in chat rooms and sending instant messages (IMs), with each subsequent message nastier than the last. As a result of complaints from Jessi and Brian, Montgomery was kicked out of some of the chat rooms, adding to his frustration and fury.

When Montgomery emailed Jessi to say he was contemplating suicide, she begged him not to and agreed to stop communicating with Brian. In turn, he threatened her with bodily harm if she continued her online romance with the younger man. She went along with Montgomery's wishes, but not for long.

Jessi craved attention, and she couldn't resist the urge to cause a little more drama. She sent Brian a message and wooed him back. When Montgomery found out, he suddenly started talking about guns and shooting sprees at work, putting his co-workers on edge. His talk of violence was so unnerving that, as a joke, a colleague arrived one morning wearing a bulletproof vest. But it was no joke when Montgomery began grilling his co-workers about Brian's work schedule.

On the morning of September 15, 2006, Jessi ignored several obscene IMs from Montgomery. When he telephoned and began screaming at her, she simply hung up. It was the last straw for Montgomery, who decided this was the day he would take charge and simplify life for Jessi and himself. He loaded his guns and, that evening, drove to Dynabrade where he waited for Brian to finish his shift. He followed him to the parking lot and, when no one was around, he shot and killed him.

Montgomery later IM'd Jessi again. "U waiting for ur bf," ["You waiting for your boyfriend?"] he wrote. No response. He IM'd her again at 2:15 AM. "come on c ur bf brian wont mind u talking to me." ["Come on, see your boyfriend Brian won't mind you talking to me."]

When investigators interviewed Brian's co-workers and began to unravel the details of the love triangle, a detective—concerned that Jessi's life might be in danger—called her in West Virginia and then contacted the local police. When an officer knocked on Jessi's front door, Shieler answered and told him her daughter wasn't expected back until later that night. The officer was suspicious, since New York State investigators said they had just spoken to the girl. After further questioning, Shieler admitted her ruse, confessing that she had been playing the role of young Jessi.

Shieler claimed that when she first visited Pogo.com, she "accidentally" used her daughter's screen name and was directed to the teen chat room. Investigators later learned she had originally registered on the site as "TallHotBlondBig50," which would have tipped most people to the fact she was a middle-aged woman. She quickly changed her screen name to "Peaches_06_17" and chatted with Montgomery and later with Brian. She claimed noble intentions, asserting she was trying to prevent Montgomery from luring teen girls online and that Brian was someone she couldn't get rid of no matter how hard she tried. The police soon learned that there was more to the story than Shieler would have them believe.

When investigators first interviewed Montgomery on September 18, he offered an alibi for the time Brian was murdered. He claimed to have gone out for dinner, returning home by 10:15 PM, which was too early to have committed the crime. But Cindy told police he hadn't gotten home until almost 11 PM, a time corroborated by cell phone records. Montgomery was placed at Dynabrade close to the time of the murder and long after he had clocked out of work.

When police broke the news to Montgomery that Jessi was actually a pudgy, 50-year-old, married mother, it didn't seem to register with him. Police described his behavior at the time as "erratic."

"He'd appear calm, then all the sudden he would get elevated, upset, stating something along the lines of, 'I just don't understand what this is all about,'" said sheriff's deputy Jason Weiss. "He was very dramatic."

"He became quiet and somewhat maudlin when he spoke of the woman and their internet relationship," according to detective Charles Tirone. As the story unfolded, the truth behind the trio's real relationship emerged. "There were hundreds of pages of chat room contact," said assistant district attorney Ken Case. "There was a lot of material. He [Montgomery] was a guy who prior to this happening was a very dedicated father. To make that much of a transformation, as a result of communicating with a fictitious person, is pretty frightening."

When police interviewed Dynabrade employees and other local witnesses, one person described seeing a man dressed in camouflage gear and a ski mask on the night of the shooting. Someone else reported hearing gunshots. In combing the crime scene, police retrieved enough evidence to bring a solid indictment against Montgomery, including a leather cartridge case with what appeared to be dog hair on it, bullet shells from a .30 caliber rifle fired at close range, and a peach pit near Brian's truck. The peach pit became a critical link to the case since it was the only piece of evidence with DNA on it. After further testing, the police found that the DNA matched the killer's.

Although he had made a confession 2 weeks after the murder, initially Montgomery refused to submit to a DNA test, but police were able to take a sample from a soda can he used and left behind after one of his police interviews. His DNA matched that on the peach pit, and Montgomery was officially arrested 2 months later, on November 27, 2006.

In July 2007, Montgomery was offered a deal of 20 years in prison for a guilty plea versus a 15- to 25-year sentence if the case went to trial and was successfully prosecuted. At first he rejected the deal, but on August 20, Montgomery pled guilty to first degree manslaughter. In spite of a later attempt to retract the plea, on November 27, he was sentenced to 20 years in prison with 5 years of post-release supervision.

Justice Penny Wolfgang delivered the sentence: "This is a totally senseless killing. This young man has been cut off in the prime of his life. … All of this for absolutely no reason."

The victim's father, when he had the opportunity to address Montgomery before sentencing, said, "My wife and I don't understand how this could happen to our family. We don't understand how such evil could exist in the world. To gun down a boy over simple jealousy does not make sense."

ABC's popular television series *20/20* aired an episode devoted to the case in March 2010. Montgomery told the news correspondent that his online relationship "became more real to me than real life. If I was smart, I would've just ended it, but it was like a drug that I needed every day."

Brian's parents filed one wrongful death lawsuit against the three they felt were responsible for their son's death: Montgomery, Shieler, and Dynabrade. They later dropped Shieler from the suit because, as Brian's dad said, "She has nothing. She's just a piece of dirt." Their case is still pending, while the haunting reality of losing a son hangs over them every day.

Brian Barrett, killed by Thomas Montgomery as the result of a twisted love triangle [Courtesy of Deb and Dan Barrett]

Montgomery after his arrest [Courtesy of Erie County Sheriff's Office]

Mary Shieler and her daughter, the real Jessi [Courtesy of Barbara Schroeder, producer of talhotblond*]*

Brian's truck at the crime scene [Courtesy of Barbara Schroeder, producer of talhotblond*]*

Dan Barrett, second from right, of Lockport, standing with his son, Daniel, during a sentencing hearing for Montgomery, seated, in the white shirt [Courtesy of Tonawanda News*]*

3

Don't Preach to Me

When Joanne Ruffner checked her email early one morning in October 2006, she discovered a surprising message waiting for her—a confirmation that she'd signed on to a swinging singles/couples website. A profile had been set up in her name, complete with personal information including her email address and IM screen name.

The About Me section was filled with intimate details that made Joanne blush. By 10 PM that night, nude photos of her had been posted on the site. By 1 AM the next morning, there were more than 16 such photos as well as a new email address with the username "joanneaznymph." Fellow swingers were encouraged to share nude photos of themselves with her. In the meantime, she soon learned that various nude photos of her were being sent to the directors of the real estate association for which she worked.

Joanne hadn't posted any of this material, but she knew who did and her immediate goal was to stop the nightmare that was unfolding before her own eyes. She recognized the photos as being taken by a former boyfriend, Mike Myers. She was in her late 20s when she met him in 2004 through a hiking group she had started on Yahoo! Groups. To get the group off to a strong start, she'd gone to Yahoo! Personals and invited other 20-somethings in the Tucson, Arizona, area to join. Though some lively discussions ensued, she never could seem to get the members together for a real hike—with the exception of Myers.

She had chatted with Myers on the phone several times before they agreed to meet for a hike. They met up at a mall in nearby Sierra Vista, where Joanne transferred her hiking gear into Myers's truck. They drove to the Coronado Cave Visitor Center before hiking to the Coronado National Monument. During the 5 hours spent together, they enjoyed each other's company and found that they seemed to have a lot in common.

"I had a boyfriend at the time," said Joanne. "Mike knew this because we talked throughout the whole hike about everything. He told me he was in his late 30s, an officer in military intelligence at Fort Huachuca in Arizona, and that he was single with no children."

Joanne felt comfortable with Myers and continued to IM with him via Yahoo! and on her cell phone. He wanted to go hiking again, but Joanne's boyfriend had become jealous of the frequent phone contact between the two and talked her out of it.

A few weeks later, Myers was transferred from Arizona's Fort Huachuca to Camp Zama in Japan. He emailed Joanne, and she confessed that she missed their conversations. When he was later deployed to Iraq, in mid-2005, he began to email her more frequently.

Joanne welcomed Myers's attention, which came during a rocky period in her relationship with her boyfriend at the time. The flirtations were innocent enough at first, but she soon sent him a few sexy photos of herself, to his obvious delight. After breaking up with her boyfriend, she lost almost all contact with Myers for more than a year. But by June 2006, she felt ready to start dating again and reached out to her erstwhile hiking buddy.

"We would spend hours on the computer chatting back and forth," said Joanne. "On his days off—Mondays—he would call me because it would be Sunday my time. We would talk for at least 2 hours at a time."

She shared every detail of her life with him, from her past relationships and childhood to her hopes and dreams. Myers seemed to reciprocate. He shared that he had two brothers; one lived in North Carolina with a wife and children, and the other, who was autistic, lived with their parents in West Virginia. He said he had been engaged once, but after realizing his fiancée only wanted him for sex and money, he had broken it off.

On June 17, 2006, Myers sent Joanne an email that changed the depth of their relationship, writing that he had been "thinking about 'our house' in West Virginia and thinking what it will be like to have you as my wife, companion, friend. I think of that a lot. I know we've kind of 'joked/hinted' at it, but I think of it a lot." By July 4, they were calling themselves a couple.

"I thought I had found my equal," said Joanne, "the one person in life that was meant for me. I thought God and my mother (who passed away in 2003) had sent him to me … he was an angel."

Since Myers was still in Iraq, they began to exchange nude photos of themselves via email and snail mail. Joanne saw no harm in it. After all, they were planning to move in together and get married.

In August 2006, they were finally together again when Myers's scheduled month of leave coincided with a conference Joanne was attending in Kansas City, Missouri. Myers told Joanne that he'd spent his first day back in the U.S. with his brother and his family in North Carolina before heading to West Virginia to go fishing with a friend. The reason she hadn't heard from him for a few days, he said, was that there was no cell phone signal where they were fishing. She believed him, of course. He called her again on his way back to North Carolina before flying to Missouri for their brief rendezvous.

They shared 3 days together in Kansas City, spending most of their time in the hotel room making love, sleeping, talking, and eating. Whenever they went out, Myers held her hand or had his arm around her waist. They appeared to be a couple who were very much in love.

Joanne was oblivious to all of the red flags that appeared along the way. Later she remembered that he'd paid for everything in cash, never with a credit card. "I didn't think anything of it at the time because some people are like that," she recalled.

Returning to North Carolina for the remainder of his R&R, Myers continued to call Joanne often. One night, he said he was at a bar with his brother and asked if she would talk to him. His brother was eager to speak to the woman who was making him so happy. Believing the man was Myers's brother, she spoke with him at length on the phone, loving the attention.

When Myers returned to Iraq in August 2006, he sent Joanne gifts: DVDs of movies he knew she liked, teddy bears, flowers, candy, and a necklace with a gold heart pendant. They set their wedding date for July 4, 2008, and she started planning the wedding.

Myers said he wanted to follow the traditional route and ask Joanne's father for her hand in marriage. He even made arrangements to go to Arizona in December 2006 to meet her father in person. In the meantime, he emailed her father to say how very much in love he was with his daughter and to thank him for raising such an amazing woman.

On August 15, Myers sent Joanne the following love letter via email. (Certain sexually explicit references have been deleted.)

> My dearest Joanne,
>
> I have never had anyone who I felt comfortable with or didn't 'make fun of me' or act like i was stupid for asking such things. That is one of the things from my past that I'm also working on. I am so happy that we are able to talk about these things, despite how difficult it is for me or you, we are doing it. Yes, it will be a slow process, but I think because of our relationship, our love and commitment to one another it will all be ok.
>
> You will get a massage anytime you want or need one. It really is a pleasure for me to do that for you. It really is relaxing for me and gives me great joy to know that it pleases you so much. And when I say 'pleases' i do not mean in a sexual way of pleasing, but in a relaxing, enjoyable way. I think it will be so relaxing to take a bath together, to just sit in the warm water and enjoy one another's company. Candles lit, sipping a glass of wine and talking about our day, our love for one another.
>
> Please don't be scared. I think you have seen that I am very easy to talk to and really like it when you do. I really like the 'assistance' and I do desire to make it 'all about you.' I'm sorry

> that it didn't seem that way in Kansas City but I really did think i was.
>
> It will just take a little time for me to learn your body and what really makes you happy. If you are happy then i am happy. I really mean that jo.
>
> I believe I told you the same thing, 'Just relax and let it happen as it does.' I want you to be relaxed with me, and i think you were; we both were very comfortable with one another. I have had two 'girl friends' cheat on me and that was devastating. I thot they loved me or at least cared about me greatly. I was wrong and my trust was greatly violated. I had told myself I will never trust another woman again, but I DO trust you 100%.
>
> I have never had a girl friend who was really beautiful like you are. I have never had anyone love me like you do. I love you so much.
>
> There have been so many times that i have been ridiculed and put down, made fun of because of my glasses, or whatever. I know that I'm not great looking, but I do try and take care of myself, best I can. I also know that you love me for who I am.
>
> I love you so much and i do trust you. I know we will have a wonderful life together. I love you joanne.

Myers sent Joanne money via PayPal to help with the wedding expenses, but then, suddenly, he told her that their plans would have to change. He said he was tired of his current work and was going to begin school in June 2007 to change his military operational status. He said he was hoping to be stationed in Texas after he finished so that they could get married and be together. Once again, she trusted him implicitly.

Though his emails continued to be filled with promises of love, Myers returned to Japan in September 2006. On October 8 of that year, he sent Joanne an email explaining what was happening in his life:

> This is the most difficult letter I will ever write. There have been so many changes in my life in

the past 4 days that I am so confused and sad, yet happy.

There are some things that I did not tell you because I never thought they would ever become an issue.

You had asked me a long time ago if I had ever been married. I misread it and thought you asked if I was married. Then you asked me a similar question again and at the time we were not 'serious' and I never thot we would ever be, so I just said no. Well, I was married some time ago and I also have two children who I have not seen in a very long time and did not ever expect to see any time soon. Well, 4 days ago they came to Japan. I was shocked, surprised, yet happy to see them after so many years. I have a daughter 16 and a son 14. It has been so hard on me. I had to take a couple days off work and have been scrambling to get into housing which fortunately was not too difficult, yet stressful. My doctor says this was not a good thing for me, but maybe it will help me. I have not been avoiding you, I just have not been online due to the move.

I'm so sorry Joanne. I love you so much, but I will not blame you if you hate me or don't want to ever talk to me again.

One other thing that surprises me is that their mother, who I have not spoken with in several years came along with them, so I have to provide her a place to stay.

I was able to get a 4-bedroom house and we are all living here together.

I'm not real happy about her being here, but have no choice in the matter.

I love you with all my heart. The doc says I probably shouldn't have made arrangements for a wedding because that has added a lot of stress on top of the PTSD [post-traumatic stress disorder]. I don't know what to do.

You have been so much of a comfort and joy to me. I love you so much.

Please forgive me. I don't know what I'm doing anymore. This deployment has wreaked havoc on my psyche and my mind. I'm not the person I was before I deployed. There were so

> many awful things I saw and was involved in over there.
>
> I'm not asking for sympathy, just for forgiveness.
>
> I love you Joanne

"I was stunned and hurt, and felt so betrayed," Joanne said. "But I thought we could work through it. I loved him enough to forgive him. He knew my past and how I had a hard time forgiving … but this time I was willing to forgive him. I wanted to be with him. He was my world, the man I was going to marry. I was just going to accept that he made a huge mistake." But he wouldn't talk to her.

Joanne was so desperate to salvage their relationship that she made plans to move to Japan to help Myers deal with his PTSD. She had the paperwork for her passport expedited and told her family, friends, and employer that she was going to Japan. On October 13, she waited for Myers to come online so she could tell him she was coming to Japan to be with him. While she was waiting, she decided to type his name into a search engine.

The first result that popped up was a photo of Myers as a U.S. Army chaplain. He had never once talked about God or the Bible with her. He had been truthful about being part of the 441st Military Intelligence Battalion, 500th Military Intelligence Brigade, but he was the chaplain, not an officer. She soon found a link to information about his daughter on a U.S. Army news website. In fact, it appeared that Myers's wife, daughter, and son had moved from Arizona to Japan with him in 2005. He had been lying the entire time.

In an email, Joanne angrily told Myers what she had discovered. Two days later, he sent her a confusing email about going to counseling with his wife. Joanne had had enough of the lies and called him in Japan. When he answered and heard her voice, he hung up, after which he emailed her, launching a flurry of messages between them. He tried to explain why he hadn't told her he was a chaplain, but none of it was making much sense. When she asked him again if he was married, his emails turned nasty.

Hurt and angry, Joanne called the base chaplain at Camp Zama on October 18. She told him everything: how she and Myers had planned on getting married, how they had been lovers, and how he never told her that he was married or a chaplain but had claimed to be a military intelligence officer. As her story unfolded, she began to realize that she had ignored all of the warning signs from the beginning.

The base chaplain told Joanne that he would talk to Myers and that the bishop for his denomination in the U.S. would be notified. Myers could lose his sponsorship with his church and be discharged from the army.

Two days later, Myers emailed Joanne and accused her of fabricating the entire story. In response, Joanne pursued the investigation with a vengeance. She sent the paperwork and the naked photos of Myers that he had emailed to her to the inspector general's office in Japan, as the office had requested. Myers continued to taunt her by email:

> Joanne, You really should go for mental health counseling. I can't believe you fabricated these emails and then of all things sent them to my supervisory chaplain. ... You really have done a mean-hearted thing to me and my family. ... On Monday I am going to JAG to see about getting a restraining order against you and try to put this scam to rest.
>
> You tell them you are my fiancée? How can that be? I never proposed. ... You are a very cruel person. ... I am so hurt that you would twist our friendship into something that it is not. Then to send those photos of when we were just playing around, wow, that is something else.

On October 26, an email from someone she didn't appear to know stopped her cold: "You will soon see photos of yourself on the internet in many compromising poses. David Chalmers." She looked at the full headers of the message and traced the email back to Japan. She knew it was Myers.

Joanne called Camp Zama to report Myers's new transgressions using the Chalmers pseudonym and about the photos of her he'd sent to a website for swingers, to friends, and even to her employer. It was obvious he was trying to get her fired. She finally admitted that Myers had a collection of nude pictures of her, which was something she had not mentioned in her initial complaint.

"Turning over those photos [to investigators] was difficult, but I didn't have any regrets," she said. She sent an email to the joanneaz nymph@yahoo.com address and wrote: "Mike, y ru doing this to me?" The person who replied claimed to know no one named Mike. But the profile of joanneaznymph on Yahoo! included a nude photo, her real name, her age, her city and state, and that she was a real estate secretary.

When Joanne contacted the swingers' website and explained that the account had been forged in her name, the proprietors asked for a copy of her photo ID to prove her identity before they would remove the profile. She followed the same procedure with Yahoo!.

"I didn't want Mike to do this to another woman," said Joanne. "Not only pretend to not be married, but to stalk them online, as well."

On November 3, Joanne's co-worker told her there were more nude photos of her on another website. A search for more resulted in a seemingly endless collection of sites displaying her profile and photos.

It was May 2007 before Joanne's persistence finally paid off. Army chaplain Myers was arrested on seven criminal charges: five for cyberstalking and one count each for adultery and conduct unbecoming an officer.

Myers pled guilty in September 2007 to all except one cyberstalking charge, which was dropped because a witness could not travel to Japan for the court martial. During the proceedings, Myers admitted his actions. "I did this with the intent to harass and cause her emotional distress by embarrassing her. … I was angry and I was hurt she had contacted my chain of command," he said. "I had already told my wife what happened. We worked things out and our relationship is really good again."

According to an eyewitness report, at the court martial, the 45-year-old Myers sobbed uncontrollably and put his head down on the defense table as the sentence was read. He was sentenced to 6 months in prison, was dismissed from the army, and received a reprimand.

"This was an individual who was a moral role model and authority figure," said major James Crawford, a Camp Zama spokesman.

"The Army does not tolerate this kind of behavior and felt it was important to prosecute."

For Joanne, it marked the end to a long fight. "I wish he'd gotten more for punishment, but it's closure," she said after the court martial. She said she had no regrets about going through with it.

Deceit comes in many forms, but when it happens as it did to Joanne, you don't expect it to be so deep and dark. "He never spoke of God," Joanne said. "I was floored. I never would have known if I hadn't caught him in his web of lies."

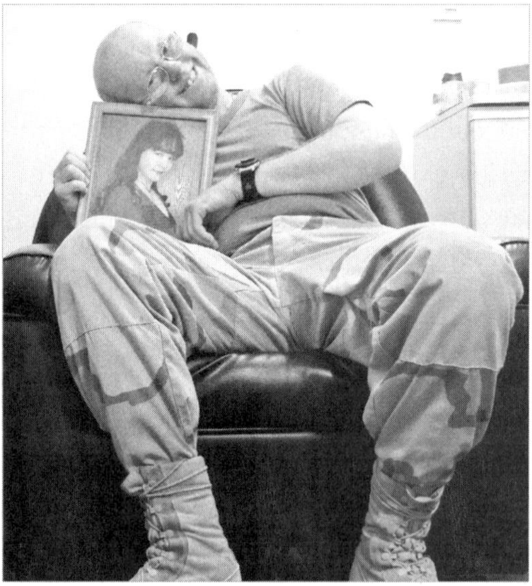

Mike Myers holding a picture of Joanne [Courtesy of Joanne Ruffner]

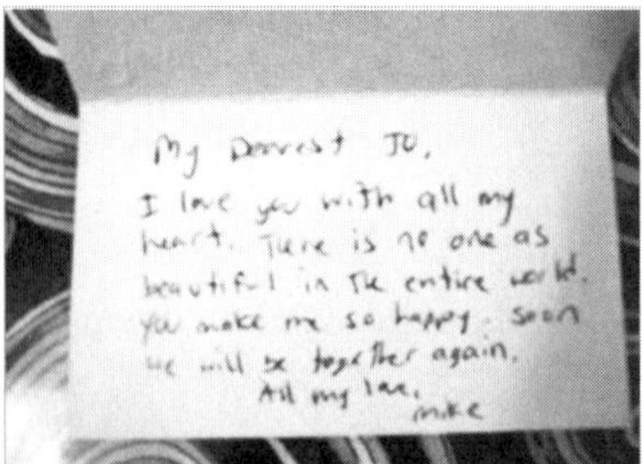

A personal note to Joanne from Myers [Courtesy of Joanne Ruffner]

Myers with Joanne Ruffner [Courtesy of Joanne Ruffner]

4

When Online Dating Victims Fight Back

"I made myself believe there had been some sort of misunderstanding and that he hadn't just raped me." With that belief, Lisa Banks stayed in a severely dysfunctional relationship for years. It would change her and her daughter's lives forever.

In the weeks leading up to the night of the rape, Lisa had been seeing a lot of her new boyfriend, Donald Brunstetter, whom she had met on an online dating site. She believed she saw all the signs of a serious relationship. They were spending every available minute together and had recently gotten to know one another's children. A few days earlier, a week after Memorial Day, Brunstetter had called to ask Lisa if she could pick up his son, Josh, at school. He suggested that Lisa bring her 6-year-old daughter, Lauren, along for the ride. Brunstetter promised he would cook dinner for all of them that evening. After dinner, they watched a movie together, during which the kids fell asleep on the couch. For Lisa, it was the ideal ending to a perfect day.

"When I indicated that I needed to load Lauren into the car to take her home, he suggested I let her sleep," she said. Brunstetter was inviting Lisa to spend the night.

"If I promise to be a complete gentleman, will you spend the rest of the night in my king-size bed with me?" was Brunstetter's polite appeal. Lisa agreed. At first, she kept her clothes on, but then he suggested she put on one of his T-shirts to be more comfortable; she agreed, and it was a decision she soon came to regret.

"If what happened next is any indication of what he meant by being 'a complete gentleman,' we were obviously operating on different wavelengths," said Lisa. "He started kissing me, then tried putting his hands under my shirt. I pushed him away and he reached into my panties. I pulled away and he crudely suggested I perform oral sex on him. When I hesitated, he simply overpowered me and had intercourse with me. He was much larger and stronger than I was, and he seemed unaware of my sincerity in asking him to stop." Since the kids were downstairs, Lisa was afraid to make any noise. Afterward, while Lisa was still reeling over the forceful encounter, Brunstetter told her he loved her. She just wasn't sure of anything anymore.

In 1998, Lisa was newly divorced and finding it difficult to juggle work, motherhood, and dating in Annapolis, Maryland. Starting over was a big challenge; she was a 36-year-old mom with a 6-year-old daughter. She had waited 2 years after her divorce before deciding it was time to take the plunge into the dating scene again. Since she and her ex-husband remained friendly, she complained to him one day about how hard it was to find a man who wanted to date a single mom.

Her ex suggested she try the free online dating site that he had recently worked on as a consultant. Lisa remembered initially thinking that any of the guys on the dating site could be an ax murderer. But she convinced herself that she could meet an ax murderer just as easily in a bar or at the public library. Besides, she felt she had a better chance of weeding out any undesirables online.

Although the website her ex recommended didn't do any background checks or verify who was posting profiles online, he reassured her that most of the users were honest people who were having a hard time meeting someone, just as she was. He laughed and said the biggest transgressions most people make on these online dating sites usually involved underestimating their weight and posting old or retouched photos of themselves. If those were the biggest challenges, Lisa felt she could deal with them.

"Initially, I went to the site to see how it worked and to see what sorts of men were listed," Lisa said. "In order to maintain control and protect my privacy, I did not post a profile of my own—at the time it was not required—but instead looked at the ads posted by men who met whatever criteria I wanted, and initiated contact with those that seemed interesting."

In March 2000, when she finally decided to post her own profile, Lisa did the smart thing. Instead of giving out her primary email address that she was given by her internet service provider (ISP), she signed up for a free email account through Hotmail. This way, she could easily delete the account if anyone she contacted got out of line. She made sure she didn't post her last name, the age or name of her daughter, or any other personal information.

"I found numerous listings for men in my area, near my age, some with children, most gainfully employed, and, based on the provided photos, not complete toads," she said.

Encouraged, she spent several hours going through the profiles. Although most of the men wrote basically the same information in their About Me sections, she ended up finding a few men who shared some commonalities with her, including a great sense of humor and a slight obsession for grammatical accuracy.

Through trial and error, she soon discovered that if you have children or pets, you should mention it early in the online dating process because it's a deal-breaker for some men. Most of the men she contacted were either single or divorced without children and had no desire to get involved with a mother of young children; even divorced dads—at least those who were divorced without custody of their children—were reluctant to date single mothers.

Lisa continued searching, and she communicated via email and IM with a few men she liked. She was always up front about the fact that she had a child.

"Many of the men I met had turned to online dating because they worked long hours or odd shifts, and some shared custody of their children," Lisa said. "Nobody seemed in a big rush to meet in person, which was quite convenient. I could get to know someone while baking cookies for the school bake sale, and it was fun having email pen pals."

Three months went by, and Lisa didn't feel as though she had made a special connection with any of the men she had gotten to know online. She gradually talked to a few of them on the phone, quickly eliminating some of them. The field finally narrowed to two men: David, who had full custody of his daughter who was about Lauren's age, and Brunstetter, whose son was also about Lauren's age and lived with his ex-wife. Both men lived in nearby towns, an added bonus.

Brunstetter would appear and chat via IM for short intervals, but he was always heading out the door on a camping or hiking trip, or to enjoy a weekend at the beach. Because he wasn't online as much as the others, Lisa found him a bit mysterious and intriguing. Although she hadn't talked with him on the phone yet, she sensed there was a strong mutual attraction developing.

Lisa decided it was time to meet both David and Brunstetter in person. Her first step was to make arrangements to meet David at one of his daughter's sporting events at a public place.

"Over the phone he seemed stable and reliable, but also overworked, tired, and disillusioned, like he never fully recovered from the failure of his marriage," said Lisa. "He was a full-time single dad, working at a demanding job 6 days a week."

The week before her arranged meeting with David, Brunstetter IM'd her and suggested they talk on the phone. She agreed. "I felt as though I had known him for years," she later recalled.

Looking back, Lisa dismissed a few red flags during their conversation, including some off-color comments he made. He often referred to himself as very handsome and said that women found him irresistible. But despite his vanity, there was still something about him she liked. He mentioned he was doing some repairs on his house that weekend and invited her to stop by. Lisa's daughter was with her father that weekend, so she accepted Brunstetter's invitation for dinner. He was going to make his famous chicken Alfredo for the two of them.

"I was a little surprised when I pulled up at the curb," said Lisa. "The house was in disrepair, and the gardens overgrown, but he'd mentioned that he was making repairs, so I assumed he'd purchased the home as a fixer-upper."

What was even more surprising was the man who answered the door. He was tall and unkempt, dressed in dirty clothes, smelled like cigarette smoke, had childhood acne scars on his face, and held a can of beer in his hand. When he smiled, she saw he was missing a few teeth. This was definitely not the handsome man he had led her to believe he was on the phone, but she shrugged off her misgivings and entered the house anyway.

When Brunstetter asked if she was willing to help him install a bathroom light fixture upstairs, Lisa was flattered. He put her right to work "as if I belonged, and a shared activity seemed a good opportunity to get acquainted." She added, "I have since learned that this is a technique typically employed by those seeking to exploit others, by creating a false sense of a shared dilemma. In fact, I now recognize many 'red flags' that I overlooked in the early stages of the relationship."

Brunstetter quickly explained why the house was so rundown. He said he had purchased it from a friend who bought foreclosed homes and residences from tax sales. He repaired them and then flipped the houses for a profit. Brunstetter had purchased his place a few years ago when he was planning on getting married. But when the relationship soured and they broke up, the house sat untouched for a while. He finally decided it was time to start fixing up the place.

While he was installing the light fixture, Brunstetter bragged about how he had paid cash for his three vehicles (a pickup truck, a Ford Bronco, and a Ford Taurus) and that he had a 19-acre parcel of land in West Virginia with a small cabin on it. He also told her how his residential power-washing business serviced upscale neighborhoods at a rate of $1,000 to $1,500 per house. Lisa was impressed.

Although they worked on the light fixture for a while, it was the wrong voltage, so Brunstetter gave up on installing it and decided to get cleaned up. Lisa went downstairs while he showered. When he came downstairs a few minutes later, Lisa was happy to see that he looked much better dressed in clean clothes. He took her on a tour of the rest of the house and even pointed out a bedroom that he said would be perfect for Lauren. Looking back, this was another red flag she missed; they weren't even dating yet, and he had their lives completely arranged. But she thought he was wonderful and decided not to say anything.

"We spent much of the afternoon talking, finding we had a lot in common, and he seemed to be a gentle and sincere person, despite his imposing physical presence," said Lisa. "He indicated that he'd placed his profile online in the hopes of finding a wife within a year's time, as he felt he was ready to settle down."

This was just what Lisa wanted to hear, red flags or not. She wanted the same thing.

Instead of Brunstetter making his famous chicken Alfredo as he had promised, they drove to a riverside bar, where he played pool while they talked. He seemed to know everyone at the bar, and by the end of the night, Lisa was euphoric and even let him kiss her. When they returned to his house, he suggested that she sleep on the sofa in the living room since it was already so late. He appeared to be sincere; he left her alone, and in the morning, they had a chance to chat a bit more. Although Brunstetter said he wanted to pursue a relationship, he didn't seem to be in any hurry to get serious. In fact, he said he wanted to date some of the other people he had met on the online dating website and encouraged her to do the same. She was surprised by his honesty but pleased that he wasn't forcing her into any commitment too quickly. She thought that maybe this could work out after all.

They talked that night on the phone, which then became their routine every night thereafter. She met David for their prearranged date but found that he was too wrapped up in his own life to make room for anyone else. Besides, she had Brunstetter now.

Just before Memorial Day, Lisa called Brunstetter and asked what his plans were for the weekend. He said one of the women he had met on the site was flying in from Chicago. Since they had made these plans before he met Lisa, Brunstetter said he had to honor his invitation. Although this woman would be staying at his house, Brunstetter told Lisa that he didn't plan on having sex with her. Lisa trusted Brunstetter wholeheartedly.

The following Monday, Brunstetter called and told Lisa he missed her. His lady friend from Chicago was long gone, and he wanted to see Lisa and even asked if he could bring his son Josh to her house for an impromptu barbecue that afternoon. Lisa was elated and thought it was perfect timing for Josh to meet Lauren. While Lisa was busy grilling burgers and making the rest of the dinner, Brunstetter played with Josh and Lauren. Though Josh seemed a bit quiet and reserved for a young boy, Lisa decided that he was just shy around strangers. Lauren liked Brunstetter right from the start.

By June 2000, Brunstetter and Lisa were spending less time at her apartment and more time at his house, and most of the time Lauren was there with them. Brunstetter came home one day and said he had hurt his back at work and needed to take some time off from his business. Lisa didn't think twice about it. In July, Josh went back to his mother's house, and Brunstetter said he could watch Lauren during the day while Lisa went to work. Lauren told Lisa that Brunstetter was fun to be with, which Lisa loved to hear. She could feel herself falling in love with him.

One weekend, Brunstetter took Lisa on an outing to his quaint cabin in West Virginia.

"It was actually a pop-up camper with a broken crank mechanism that had been tied to a tree to keep the canvas up," she said. "There was no plumbing or power, the canvas was torn; it was infested with bees and ants, and had clearly provided a cozy winter home for small woodland creatures."

Brunstetter explained that the camper was just a temporary place and that he planned on building a house just for her. He called her his true love. She was captivated and believed him, of course.

Then, he began pressuring her about getting married. It would be best to get married before September, he said. That way, Lisa could enroll Lauren in school in his district so she wouldn't have to change schools later on.

While this made sense to Lisa, Brunstetter began to express some rather unusual ideas about marriage. He said he wanted their marriage to be open so he could explore his sexuality with others. He said he needed to have sex with someone else—with or without Lisa—a few times a year. If she couldn't agree to that, he said their relationship would have to end.

Lisa was devastated. She couldn't agree to those terms, and she told him so. They didn't talk about it any further, but by the end of the day, Brunstetter's attitude had changed completely; he said he intended to be 100 percent faithful to Lisa.

"I thought he had been pulling my leg the whole time, just to see how I'd react," she said. "It had to be a joke, right?"

On August 14, 2000, Brunstetter and Lisa were married. Brunstetter chose the date because he said it was exactly 6 months before and after Valentine's Day. Lisa thought this was the most romantic thing she had ever heard, but her happiness didn't last long.

"Donnie often commented on how attractive he found almost every woman he met, suggesting frequently that we take one to bed with us," said Lisa. "Even on our honeymoon, he kept bringing this up. He even joked that when Lauren turned 18 that he would divorce me and marry her."

Lisa didn't take him seriously. Brunstetter never went back to work during the time they were married. All he did was care for Lauren while Lisa was at work. He made sure Lauren ate breakfast, went to school, and returned home safely. During the summer, he spent all day with Lauren. Lisa felt this was totally acceptable behavior for a stepfather, especially since he wasn't working.

But the longer Brunstetter was unemployed, the more of a toll it took on their marriage. He never applied for or received unemployment, Social Security, or any other disability assistance to help out financially. He had lofty ideas for business ventures. At one point, he announced his intention to become a limo driver, but Lisa soon discovered he had DUIs, suspensions, and moving violations on his driving record, precluding any such employment. Another time, he said he wanted to work as a locksmith, but it came out that he had been convicted of breaking and entering and that idea quickly fizzled. He even suggested selling Lauren's used underwear on eBay. Lisa thought he was joking but later realized that she should have seen this as a red flag, too. The couple began arguing more and more. Finally, Lisa couldn't take it any longer and, in 2002, she left him. Their divorce was finalized on November 27, 2002.

Lisa started to rebuild her life with Lauren, who was then 11 years old. By the time of Lauren's 14th birthday, in 2005, Lisa discovered that Lauren had been cutting herself with razor blades.

"I was shocked, frightened, and confused," Lisa said. "I got her into therapy, and 9 months later she admitted that Brunstetter had sexually abused her from the very beginning. I was simultaneously angry at the monster that had mutilated my child and devastated for my injured daughter. I was sure she intended to kill herself."

Later that year, Lisa enrolled Lauren in a program designed to help children who have been sexually molested, and over time, the teenager began to heal. Lisa filed charges against Brunstetter in September 2007.

In her impact statement at the trial in July 2008, 17-year-old Lauren offered the following testimony to the court:

> My mother tells me stories of a younger Lauren, a person I can't find anymore. If Donnie had never done what he did, things might be different. I watched my mother's heart break when she learned what he had done to me and believed she should somehow have known about it and made it stop. The things that happened to me when I was 8, 9 and 10 years old were things I was powerless to stop. I now see that Donnie didn't love my mom and he didn't love me. He was using my mom to get to me and using me to satisfy his perverted desires. None of this was my fault, or my mom's fault, and it's time for Donnie to pay for all the suffering he has put us through. Because of what Donnie did to me I have had a lot of problems to deal with. I have countless emotional, mental and physical scars. I have experienced things that no innocent child should have to deal with. I am not a kid anymore, and I haven't been in a long, long time. I was introduced to adult experiences I did not understand in a way that was absolutely wrong. I am suspicious of people who try to befriend me. I don't know who I can trust. And I feel like everyone who meets me can tell I am different and thinks less of me as a result. I want Donnie Brunstetter to be in a place where he can't hurt anyone else.

Brunstetter was sentenced on August 20, 2008. Of the 15 charges brought against him, he was found guilty of six: two charges of child abuse, unnatural or perverted practice; second degree sex offense; third degree sex offense; and second degree assault. He received 15 years in prison, most of which were suspended; he still had to serve 5 years of his sentence. He was also required to register as a sex offender and to pay court costs.

Brunstetter tried to get his sentence reduced and the charges against him dismissed. His requests continued through October 2009, but on November 2, the state attorney's office called Lisa to advise her that Brunstetter had changed his mind about the appeal.

"Donald wrote a letter to the judge admitting his guilt and withdrew his appeal," said Lisa. "He requested that a copy be sent to me and to my daughter, as he expressed his remorse for the abuse and stated clearly that none of what happened was her fault and that he hoped she would continue to get the counseling she needs to move past this."

Lisa and Lauren both remain in therapy and continue their efforts to put the past behind them. According to Lisa, she intends to remain single.

ANNE ARUNDEL POLICE DEPARTMENT
BRUNSTETTER, DONALD SCOTT

Aliases/Monikers:

Book Date: 08-21-2007

Hair: BROWN
Eyes: BLUE
Height: 602
Weight: 220
Build:
Race: WHITE
Sex: MALE
DOB: 08-29-1963
Skin: MEDIUM
Tattoos, Physical Oddities, Etc:

Donald Scott Brunstetter after he was finally charged with sexually abusing his stepdaugher [Courtesy of Anne Arundel County Police Department]

5

Just Trying to Help a Friend

Anonymous: "Amy L, is the one I love ... Amy L is the one I love."

Jojobriggs: "And Amy, I know you for the fake kind dirty slut you really are, remember that."

Funfunfun: "So Amy you still sleeping around with your best friends men and trying to deny it or your own family members?"

Anonymous: "do not worry Amy this is all being said for your own good and betterment of yourself."

JohnBradshawLayfiend: "Amy I love you. By god you are the sexies thing ever invented."

Lola: "Go to hell along with Ame L she is a peace of crap."

In May 2004, the comments on Amy Lawson's blog arrived in quick succession, and all of them originated from the same IP address. She knew who it was and wondered when the harassment would ever end.

It was only 3 years earlier that Amy had been an outgoing high school junior in coastal Connecticut. In June 2001, one of Amy's friends complained that someone—she assumed it was a man—was harassing her, constantly sending IMs. Amy decided to help her friend by sending an IM to this annoying pest, whose screen name was "Fink," asking him to stop IMing her friend. Her request was polite but firm, and Fink did as she asked. But then he channeled all of his attention to Amy instead.

For the next 3 years, Amy was inundated with dozens of IMs every day from Fink. Since she used her full name as her screen name, it was easy for Fink to find her home address by searching the white pages online. At first, he sent gifts to her home: a teddy bear, flowers, cards. She quickly threw them away.

Later that summer when she went to the local gas station, a young male attendant about her age came over to her car to pump gas and began talking to her.

"You're Amy, right?" he asked. Amy was puzzled for a moment until he introduced himself as Fink. She could hardly wait to leave. But before she could, Fink tried to give her a DVD. She handed it back to him, saying that she wasn't interested, and drove away. Fink then started sending love letters to her home address. Again, she threw them away. When Amy graduated from high school in June 2002, Fink sent her a $100 money order through the mail as a graduation present. Amy sent it back to Fink; he returned it, and she sent it back to him again. But he was unrelenting: He sent it to Amy one more time, at which point she simply tossed the check on the end table in the living room. Finally, Amy's mother found it, saw who it was from, and knowing Fink had been harassing Amy, promptly threw it in the trash.

Amy blocked all the IM screen names that she knew Fink had created and politely asked him to leave her alone. But he still wouldn't take no for an answer. There were some weeks when there were no IMs, and then suddenly, he would send more IMs under a new screen name. His IMs and emails continued even after she moved to San Diego to start college in August 2003.

In May 2004, Fink's IMs suddenly stopped. Amy thought the entire ordeal was over. She believed Fink had finally moved on, so she breathed a sigh of relief. But her joy was short-lived. Fink simply changed online mediums and started to post comments on her blog instead:

Bjbob899: maybe your just a spick now like your boyfriend

Bjbob899: dirty whore

Bjbob899: i was promised a blow job

AmyL: please stop Iming me

Bjbob899: you promised me a blow job at a race

AmyL: please stop IMing me

Bjbob899: So the blow job offer was a hustle?

AmyL: please stop IMing me

Bjbob899: ok white girl you win..Boy buy

Fink tracked down Amy's boyfriend's email address and began harassing him in hopes that he would ask Amy to respond.

When his appeals to Amy's boyfriend went unheeded, Fink opened an account on the blog-hosting site LiveJournal and began posting an unrelenting stream of entries professing his love for Amy, all while she kept asking him to stop. On May 18, 2004, one of Fink's posts made Amy very uneasy. Fink began talking about her parents' house: "Can anybody say Egging a certain house on Geer ave [Amy's parents lived on Geer Avenue] on video? Speaking of Geer ave this brings me to something I want to say about a former friend of mine named Amy L … I never judged you one bit you dirty rotten skank now did i? Amy your not even worth the bandwidth this fuckin journal is written on."

That evening, Fink hammered away at Amy with IMs from four different screen names. But this time, the tone of his IMs began to frighten her:

6:46:18 PM: Amy what happens to your parents house tonight I am not responsible for

6:47:40 PM: you intruded in my life for the last time you cruel psychopathic bitch

6:49:33 PM: just for the record I feel bad about your parents house but you made it personal not me

6:53:55 PM: Look Aimee I am sorry I can not change the past

6:54:45 PM: This hurts me more then it hurts you

6:55:27 PM: But we both realiise what you did to me was screwed up

6:56:43 PM: Amy do you not care about anything

6:57:28 PM: lol I threten to do something to your parents house and you do not care lol ... some daughter you are

6:58:24 PM: all's i want is an appology

7:03:50 PM: Amy

7:03:51 PM: Amy

7:03:53 PM: Amy

7:03:54 PM: Amy

7:04:15 PM: Amy

7:10:20 PM: I am sorry

7:10:28 PM: I love you always have always will

7:13:27 PM: we used to be best friends ... what changed

7:15:18 PM: Amy I am offering to stop

7:16:35 PM: All's I want is an ppology

Amy reread one of his comments in sheer disbelief: "I love you always have always will."

"Those were pretty deep feelings for someone who knows me in no greater detail than having pumped my gas one time," she said. "I wanted to call the police before this, but to be honest, I wasn't sure they would consider him sending me gifts enough to arrest him for stalking. I had no idea it would get to this point."

The next day, Amy's father, Bryan, went to the local police department and filed a complaint on Amy's behalf. He told the police about the online harassment she was enduring, how she was frightened, and how Fink had threatened to damage her parents' house. The officer assigned to the case asked Amy to fax any relevant information directly to him.

"Within 24 hours, the officer was holding 25 pages of conversations, away messages, etc. that showed Fink had been harassing me," Amy said. She was elated when the police officer called her with news that an arrest warrant for Fink was being issued and that an officer had warned Fink in person to stop harassing Amy.

But Fink didn't like the police appearing on his doorstep. He didn't waste any time posting his thoughts on LiveJournal the next day:

> I took something wayyyyyy too far yesterday and I would like to apologise. Yes cops showed up at my door at midnight yesterday to warn me, and yes I was shocked. I thretned to egg somebodies parents house ... Keep in mind these were threats made online and had no real merit. But anyway was I immature in making them? Yes I was. Did I take things with Amy to far? Yes I did. Amy and I used to be really good friends ... And if you do not like that Bow wow wow and kiss my ass.

Fink continued to post his heartfelt feelings for Amy, while she simply waited for the police to arrest him.

On May 24, Fink posted the following entry: "I am not mad at Amy for calling the cops on me even though she lives in california now and I in ct. . .It makes me mad that as a Tax payer Police are responding to such bullshit calls when somebody was murdered here last week. Amy lives in California and since I did not make the threat to her parents directly it is not considered thetening and plus there has to be reason to belive that I was serious with the threat which I obvisoely was not."

The officer assigned to Amy's case told her to remove Fink from her IM buddy list and to ignore him, which she did. But as she discovered more background information about Fink, her worries intensified.

Amy began to suspect that the police didn't think Fink was a direct threat to her because she was in California. Her friends on the East Coast did some research on Fink, whose full name was Franklin Fink, and discovered a long list of arrests. In 1999, Fink was arrested and convicted for harassing and threatening a girl. He received 1 year of probation. In 2001, he was arrested again for breach of peace, harassment, threatening, and computer crime. He was convicted on five of seven charges and received 3 years of probation, but his sentence was suspended. Amy knew that the police department was well aware of Fink's past activities, but she didn't know why they weren't doing anything to help her.

"I was scared of [him]," she said.

When Fink posted that he had sold his hard drive, Amy called the officer assigned to her case, telling him that this was Fink's attempt to discard any incriminating evidence. The officer just said that Fink probably responded that way "since I scared him into thinking we would take his computer away from him that first night we went over there."

Amy didn't know what to think or believe. One minute she was angry; the next she was just plain frightened. "His actions and words placed me in severe emotional distress and put me in fear, not only of my own well-being, but that of my family back home," she said. "I did not want to simply 'forgive and forget' these incidents. If I moved on with my life, and ignored Fink's actions, I knew that I would be leaving the door open for other women and girls to fall prey to this bully."

A few days later, on May 29, Amy's father went to the gas station where Fink worked and confronted him in person. Amy's father told Fink to leave his family alone, and if Fink didn't, he would return with the police officer on the case. Fink's LiveJournal post 4 days later revealed Fink's darker side: "I had one hand banging on the counter and my other clinching a boxcutter in my pocket since I was contemplating either punching the guy right then and there or even stabbing him."

"Honestly, I have never spoken to someone or seen anyone whose train of thought was more … disheveled," Amy said.

Amy began filing complaints everywhere: AOL Instant Messenger, LiveJournal, Fink's ISP, and Yahoo! (the host for the email accounts through which he harassed her). She also kept contacting the officer handling her case.

By June 16, Amy's mother told her that there was a signed arrest warrant against Fink, but it could take up to 3 weeks to grant it even if the judge found probable cause.

An officer from the Connecticut State Police called Amy the next day. She had sent them information about her case and plenty of background on Fink's prior arrests. According to the state trooper who called her, Fink was still on probation, and online harassment was a violation of his probation. The trooper didn't think it would be hard to charge Fink on those grounds. Although Amy was excited when she hung up the phone, nothing happened.

On June 26, Amy was still waiting for the arrest warrant to be issued, and Fink was posting on LiveJournal that he was the person being wronged and asked why Amy was blaming him.

"I sat there crying, because he made me so mad," said Amy. "He makes this seem as if he had done nothing wrong, when it was pretty damn obvious that he had. He had no right to do this to me—make me upset, make me sad, make me doubt myself."

On July 2, Amy returned to Connecticut to visit her family and discovered that Fink had been arrested the night before.

Fink's court date for Amy's online harassment case was set for July 15. Amy and her sister went to the courthouse, but Fink didn't show up. A bail letter was mailed to him, notifying him that he had to appear for the rescheduled court date of August 4 or face the consequences.

Fink began to IM Amy again:

> "I love you why wont you say anything"
>
> "Dirty whore"
>
> "Amy I just have one thing to say ... I am sorry you waisted a whole day for me ... And This jury trial thing that your about to be summoned for I have nothing to do with ... Nothing personal I hate dragging your name threw the mud but I have no choice. So it's not personal ... I am sorry. thats all I wanted to say good bye"

On August 3, Amy talked to the head of probation in Litchfield County in Connecticut, where Fink had previously been arrested. He told Amy that Fink was just trying to control her and her emotions.

The next day, which was Fink's rescheduled court date, the prosecutor's office called Amy. Fink claimed that he had not been online since he had been arrested and had not contacted Amy. But the prosecutor produced copies of the IMs that Fink had actually been sending her. The prosecutor told Amy, "We're going to raise his bail because … he's kind of a weird little guy."

"*Kinda* weird?" Amy said.

"All right, he's a weird guy," the prosecutor said.

On August 13, Fink's bail was increased from $10,000 to $45,000, which his family couldn't post. The state attorney told Amy that they "slapped the golden bracelets" on him and put him in a jail cell. Fink spent 1 month in jail and finally pled guilty to the charges. However, he did not receive any additional jail time. The court simply restricted his internet use and ordered him to undergo psychological counseling. His computer was also confiscated, and his ISP account was canceled, along with his LiveJournal and Yahoo! accounts.

And Amy? She's married now with a family. She endured years of harassment from Fink, but her persistence paid off. Her ordeal is finally over.

Amy Lawson (with her father, Bryan), harassed after trying to help a friend [Courtesy of Amy Caruso]

Franklin Fink, who finally stopped harassing Amy after many years [Courtesy of Norwich Police Department]

6

Stalking Ghosts

At first, Jason Hawes shrugged off the strange emails from a man named Joseph Kennedy as the rantings of some nut. Not many people would mess with then 36-year-old Jason, a formidable man with a muscular build. But as Jason discovered, this was no ordinary nut; this was an online stalker who would soon begin threatening his wife and children:

> Ho! Ho! Ho! Did you think I was gone forever??? No such luck. I just got out of the Cook County Jail after 2 months in HELL. I am sending this BCC to prevent all of you from contacting one another and comparing notes. I hope and pray that OSAMA BIN LADEN KILLS THOUSANDS of Americans this Spring!!! I also hope and pray that a TERRIBLE EARTHQUAKE OCCURS OR A MASSIVE VOLCANIC ERUPTION KILLS THOUSANDS!!! Last night I MURDERED a young, pretty woman after raping her several times. I killed her by strangling her with a pair of her brown-colored pantyhose!!! You are next VERENE!!!
> Until later SCUM!!!
>
> A Serial Killer

In 1990, Jason and his buddy Grant Wilson co-founded a ghost-hunting organization called The Atlantic Paranormal Society (TAPS) in Warwick, Rhode Island. Both men claimed to have experienced paranormal events and were interested in learning more. By day, they were plumbers for Roto-Rooter; by night, they looked for ghosts. As more members joined TAPS, Jason's and Grant's reputations as ghost hunters began to grow and, in 2003, the Syfy cable channel asked the duo if they would be interested in filming a television series based on their paranormal investigations. In October 2004, Syfy aired the first episode of the *Ghost Hunters* series, which has since earned a cult following among those who love all things paranormal.

In March 2005, Jason and other members of TAPS started to receive disturbing emails from someone who called himself a serial (sometimes "cereal") killer. At first, Jason and the staff at TAPS deleted the emails, but the emails continued to pour into their inboxes, and the threats escalated:

> From: Sharon Edwards
> <womanly9988@yahoo.com>
>
> To: TAPS Members
>
> Sent: Saturday, March 12, 2005 4:02 PM
>
> Subject: Thank You
>
> The Kennedys are FILTH and SCUM!!! Swimming in Shark-Infested Waters is nothing compared to what I am going to do to you before I MURDER YOU!!! Ho! Ho! Ho! I Murdered another Young Woman last night. That's 3 so far this year. [F—-] YOU F.B.I.!!!

> From: Gomez Fuentes
> <dancin_mexcan@yahoo.com>
>
> To: TAPS members
>
> Sent: Tuesday, March 15, 2005 12:02 PM
>
> Subject: Mexico
>
> Well. I have another short stay in the Cook County Jail ahead of me. I am not looking forward to it but I get my Revenge on Young Women. By the way, this missive is being sent BCC to 7 TAPS members and 7 Non-TAPS members, including one of my "friends" in Australia. VERENE-I hope and pray that GOLDA and MOSHE are both DEAD by now or at least DYING of CANCER!!! BENJAMIN

R.-Have you RAPED any FEMALE WHITE BUFFALOES lately? CYTOCOP-I posted another message at VJ claiming to be a Desparate Young Woman!!! I got some great responses from new VICTIMS!!! ... Want to hear a good joke? What did the Penus say to the Vagina??? Answer-"Can I squirt sperm inside you?" Ho! Ho! Ho! Attention F.B.I,-I am a Genius and infinitely too smart for you to catch because 1. I ONLY use a Library Computer. 2. I ONLY use Free Yahoo Mail. 3. I NEVER use the same e-mail address TWICE. 4. I ONLY use HACKED Library Card Numbers to log onto the Internet. 5. I provide False Clues like the Cook County Jail. 6. I have a GENIUS I.Q. of 162. 7. I know NONE of the people I Terrorize. I hope and pray that Osama Bin Laden KILLS THOUSANDS of Americans this JULY 17!!! TONIGHT I MURDER another Young Woman whom I have been Stalking for 2 weeks. She wears Brown-colored Pantyhose and that gives me a HUGE Erection!!! Shalom. A Serial Killer

The staff at TAPS continued to receive the strange emails, but the team refused to respond.

"The problem is I [had] no issues with anyone that I [knew] of," said Jason. "I felt it would give him the attention he wanted if I responded, so I never have." But then, the emails began to focus directly on Jason's wife, Kris Hawes, and their children.

From: Efrem Zimbalist Jr.
<spanish_dandy@yahoo.com>

To: TAPS members

Sent: Saturday, April 09, 2005 12:31 PM

Subject: Hardee's On Brayton Road

Hello from the very nice Warwick Public Library at 600 Sandy Lane. Your library does not have as many Computers as the one I go to near Wrigley Field but they are Private and the Basthroom is Clean. Jason Hawes-Shame On You for Blocking Your E.M. Address!!! I guess I will have to come visit you and Kris and your Children at [address deleted for privacy] or Call you at [phone number deleted for privacy]. After Breakfast at the Dunkin' Donuts, I paid a visit to the T.A.P.S. Trailer HQ that I have seen so many times on Television. How Quaint! I am eating Lunch at Hardee's after I send this missive to all my many BCC acquaintances. TERRI -I apologize for forgetting to send you any personal messages lately. I posted 3 Messages at Goldsmith Students. Can you spot them??? Attention F.B.I.-Did you get the reference to Inspector Erskine. If you're still in the Dark, just check out Efrem Zimbalist Jr. the Actor. CYTOCOP-There is still one of my FAKE messages posted at VJ. It is dated 3-7 and is from a "desparate young woman" names Alicia C. I got some good responses to that. Hey F.B.I....Am I from Chicago or not??? Ho! Ho! Ho! I will be watching my favorite TV show Ghost Hunters this July and also my 2nd favorite show-Battlestar Galactica. I hope that Commander Adama Lives! My dear brother Osama will SLAUGHTER THOUSANDS of Americans on JULY 17. I will both RAPE and SLAUGHTER AMY by my 40th Birthday on April 15. Soon I will have a 5th pair of Pantyhose in my Shoebox. Kris Hawes MAY be Number 6. Ho! Ho! Ho!Because of my GENIUS I.Q. of 162, I can NEVER be caught. I will be on RED ALERT for a Police StakeOut of the Warwick Library, Hardee's, Dunkin' Donuts, etc!!! AMY, soon I will take a pair of Silky Pantyhose from YOUR Lingerie drawer!!! Get your Vagina and Breasts ready for ME YOU FILTHY BITCH!!!

aurevoir,

the Cereal Killer

From: Miriam Sawyer <feminine8@yahoo.com>

To: TAPS Members

Sent: Tuesday, April 12, 2005 10:33 AM

Subject: T.A.P.S. Membership

Ode To Murder

Amy I can't find your address

So this is your lucky day more or less.

A young virgin I won't be able to Rape and Kill

If you need a Shrink after this send me the Bill.

KRIS HAWES will be taking your place

I can;t wait to meet her face to face.

When Jason leaves Warwick to hunt a Ghost

Of our time alone together I'll make the most.

To [address removed for privacy] I will go

There Naked in Bed Together KRIS and I will put on a show. ...

My 12 inch Penus will Penetrate her Vagina

With Vaseline Galore as an oily liner.

I'll RAPE and then KILL KRIS while she Cries

Then I'm off to Hardee's for a burger and fries.

A 5th pair of Pantyhose for my Shoebox

Then the countdown to Murder 6 while the clock tick tocks.

The F.B.I. and Police are in Darkness with NO Clues

When you take on an I.Q. of 162 you are bound to lose.

My brother OSAMA on JULY 17 will Strike

The BLOODY Pictures on CNN I will truly LIKE.

I'm getting a Job in WARWICK and staying here

Where [address removed for privacy] is so very near.

Goodbye Elgin, Geneva, Batavia, Fox River Valley

In Warwick, what will be my final Murder Tally?

Shalom,
Osama Jr.

> P.S. Hey F.B.I.-Do you really think I would use a Computer at the Warwick Public Library and then be Stupid enough to tell you? Where am I using a Computer? Ho! Ho! Ho1

As the content of the emails escalated and grew more bizarre, Jason contacted the local police, who in turn contacted the FBI because of the death threats and self-professed claims that the cyberstalker was a serial killer.

Whoever the cyberstalker was, he was clever. He would open a free email account on Yahoo!, send one message to the intended recipients, and then cancel the account. When the cyberstalker sent the next message, he used a new Yahoo! email account and then deleted it after he sent the email. He hoped to confuse the police and FBI, but opening and closing free email accounts doesn't safeguard a user's anonymity.

The FBI told Jason that the email threats had been traced to an ISP somewhere in Ohio. Jason wanted to speed up the pace of the investigation, so he contacted the online safety organization WHOA. After he forwarded several emails to WHOA, he discovered that although the FBI was correct that the ISP headquarters were in Ohio, that's not where the messages originated.

Email message headers (e.g., To, From, Date, Subject) provide plenty of hidden clues, but there's a way to display these full headers to retrieve all of the behind-the-scenes information. When the message header is properly displayed, the message can then be traced to the specific ISP/location by looking at the originating internet protocol (IP) address, which consists of four sets of numbers that have one to three numerals in each set. Each IP address is unique and assigned to a specific computer/account.

WHOA determined within a day that the messages to Jason had come from two IP addresses: 216.183.185.70 and 216.183.185.133.

This data helped pinpoint the IP addresses where the messages originated. The messages were sent from two libraries in the Pittsburgh area: the Bethel Park Public Library and Mt. Lebanon Public Library. Both used the same Expedient Communications ISP in Cleveland, Ohio.

When Jason passed this information along to the FBI, the FBI discovered that the cyberstalker was using a third IP address at the Upper St. Clair Library, also in the Pittsburgh area. Since these libraries did not have any video cameras or sign in/sign out logs for anyone using library computers, the FBI had to find another way to figure out who was sending the emails.

On April 19, the FBI took control of Jason's email account after he received the following messages from the cyberstalker:

> From: Sonny Garfunkel
> <sonnyboy6644@yahoo.com>
>
> To: Jason Hawes
>
> Sent: Tuesday, April 19, 2005 11:10 AM
>
> Subject: Providence Haunting
>
> Funeral Verses
>
> Last night I Murdered Victim Number 5
>
> She's Dead and Buried, that ain't no Jive.
>
> 5 pair of Pantyhose for my Shoebox
>
> Kris Hawes is next, Tick Tock Tick Tock.
>
> East, West, North, South from Warwick you go
>
> A 100 mile radius to search to and fro.
>
> I Buried her Corpse in a woods dark and deep
>
> Her Silky Brown Pantyhose are now mine to keep.
>
> She Cried and Sobbed and Begged for her life
>
> I Laughed and Slit her Throat with my Knife. ...
>
> I Raped her 2 times and made her Spread her Legs Wide
>
> Her Vagina was all Hot and Oily inside.
>
> I've got her Purse, Credit Cards and Money
>
> When I think of her Dying Sobs it sure is Funny.
>
> The Quantico Profiler says I'm filled with such Hate

That venting my Murderous impulses feels great.

Library Computers and Free Yahoo Mail

Putting the Cuffs on me will be to no avail.

The Quantico Profiler says I'm on a vast stage

My 13 BCCs let me vent all my Rage.

The F.B.I. can't catch me because I'm too damn smart

an I.Q. of 162 for a start.

In Warwick I've got a job and sublet

To [address deleted for privacy] I can easily get.

Kris Hawes Breasts and Vagina soon will be mine

I know Raping her wil be quite fine.

I'll Kill Jason's Kris while she Sobs and Cries

Then it's McDonald's for a Burger and Fries.

Reanna W., Paula D., Donna L. you're all on my list

Your Throats I will Strangle after your Vaginas I Kiss.

Cantigny World War 1 Memorial was a favorite spot

Can you track down this clue F.B.I.? Why not give it a shot?

A Jumbo bag of Doritos and a 6 Pack of Coca-Cola I will need

Watching CNNs Bloody Pictures on JULY 17...indeed!

My Sociopath Rage is all I.D.O.C.s fault

Illinois gave me 5-Felonious Assault.

Kill! Kill! Kill! Kill! God Damn It! Shut Up!

Which Young Woman will next Drink from my Bloody Cup?

Aurevoir,
The Cereal Killer

From: Patricia Donovan
<preg_womn@yahoo.com>

To: Jason Hawes

Subject: Message Board

This letter is for the F.B.I.

If you wish to establish 2 way contact with me, post a message on the Message Board at www.goldsmithstudents.com. Terri is the Webmaster. Her e-mail address is [address removed for privacy]. Her Phone Number and Address are listed in Yahoo People Search. You might want to tell her what you are doing and also tell her not to delete my response. When you contact me, be sure to include a valid F.B.I..e-mail address so I can be sure that Jason or Grant are not answering me. I will only use the F.B.I. e-mail address for verification purposes, as I am not sure you cannot Trace me from an F.B.I. Website. I will post a Message at Goldsmith Students in response to you and we can have an ongoing discourse that way. Of course, I realize that many T.A.P.S. members will take a "peek" at our exchanges. If you do NOT choose to correspond with me, I will Murder another young woman this Friday night. This is your ONE opportunity.

Aurevoir,
The Cereal Killer

By watching the flow of emails, the FBI was able to find a pattern in the days of the week, the time of day, and where the messages originated. "One FBI agent had a BlackBerry and was watching the emails as they came in," Jason said. "The agents involved in the case watched this gentleman email me and were building a strong case against him. This idiot ended up emailing all the government branches, including the Secret Service, telling them I wanted to take out the president. A Secret Service agent came to my house to interview me because of those emails. I know he was doing his job and I respect that. It's just strange having to deal with that because of this idiot."

In a joint effort, the Secret Service, the FBI, and the Bethel Park Police Department monitored the three libraries to nab the cyberstalker. They didn't have to wait long. On May 14, Barry Clinton Eckstrom was arrested at the Bethel Park Public Library for threatening to kill the president and threatening to shoot Roto-Rooter employees. The 51-year-old Eckstrom from Upper St. Clair was sitting at a computer typing while an FBI agent sat at the computer next to him. The agent watched as Eckstrom typed an email to the Department of Homeland Security that had been forged in Jason's name: "I hate and despise the scum President Bush! I am going to kill him in June on his father's birthday."

At the initial court hearing on May 16, 2 weeks after he had been arrested, Eckstrom told the magistrate that he had only "typed in another person's name" and then was told not to make any other comments until a lawyer could be appointed to represent him. Witnesses at the hearing said that Eckstrom was so skinny that his jail uniform pants fell to his ankles at one point. It turned out he was unemployed and living with his parents.

On October 20, Eckstrom pled guilty in federal court to the charge of making a threat against the U.S. president. The hearing for his sentencing was set for January 5, 2006.

Jason made sure he attended the sentencing to provide a victim impact statement. He later remarked that he was glad he was there.

"They were going to let him off on just probation," Jason said, shaking his head. "But because I was able to tell the court what happened and how it affected me and my family, they gave him 2 years in federal prison, 3 years' probation with an ankle bracelet, and he is not allowed to use a computer or any electronic storage device during that time." The judge also ordered Eckstrom to undergo psychiatric treatment while serving his time in prison.

In August 2009, Eckstrom was released into the custody of his brother and was not allowed to use a phone or computer for 3 years while on probation.

While Jason and his family have since moved to another city in Rhode Island, he and Grant have continued their successful partnership with the *Ghost Hunters* (even though Grant left the show in

2011) and *Ghost Hunters International* TV shows (and specials) on the Syfy Channel. They have published books about their paranormal exploits and currently offer special ghost-hunting packages at The Spalding Inn in Whitefield, New Hampshire, which they purchased in 2009. In the meantime, it appears that at least one ghost from Jason's past is gone for good.

Jason Hawes (with his dog, Maddie), whose fame resulted in email threats directed at his family [Courtesy of Jason Hawes]

7

How to Catch 700 Online Sexual Predators

Most people knew Tennessee resident Royal Raymond Weller, 49, by his online handle of "G.O.D." As host of the Kids the Light of Our Lives website, Weller shared his collection of child pornography with his online congregation of more than 700 pedophiles.

"You could go and if you were in the club, arrange a time and a place when online you could view a child being raped and brutalized in real time," said Jim Gamble, chief executive of Britain's Child Exploitation and Online Protection (CEOP) Centre.

The photos were heartbreaking. The live streaming videos, basically "on-demand" sexual molestation, were the worst. Babies as young as a few months old were victims. Investigators involved with one of the world's largest online child pornography stings still can't get the images out of their minds.

The case, later named Project Wickerman, began in 2005 in Edmonton, Alberta, Canada, in a jail cell. A prisoner wanted to make a deal by trading his online contacts for some in-prison perks. The investigation soon moved east where Toronto police discovered the Kids the Light of Our Lives chat room. After the initial investigation, Canadian authorities from the Virtual Global Taskforce believed the child pornography network was big—very big. In turn, the Canadian authorities informed the British police, who also began to gather evidence and work with law enforcement agencies around the world. In March 2006, Weller was arrested along with more than 40 other people, but the online horror didn't stop.

Within a week after the arrests, the chat room was back in service, hosted by "Son-Of-God."

Sgt. Paul Krawczyk, then an undercover detective with the Toronto Police Service's Child Exploitation Section, joined the chat room after Weller's arrest, using a pseudonym to track the online users who frequented the site. Within a week, Krawczyk had gained the trust of everyone there, including Son-Of-God.

"They thought police had done their case and wouldn't be following them, but at the same time they were really careful," he said. Krawczyk fit in so well with the group that the members of the network appointed him the "bouncer" for the chat room.

"They actually gave administrative powers to the only cop in the room," he said. "It gave me power to vet members—but I didn't want to kick people out of the room. I wanted them to come in and be welcome so we could arrest them. It gave me the power to be able to trace the members. That's why we wanted this power and they gave it to us on a silver platter. And I was sitting there the whole time saying: 'You don't know what you're getting into.'"

Before long, Krawczyk discovered that Son-Of-God lived in Britain, which fueled the start of the investigation in England. On September 28, 2006, the CEOP arrested 27-year-old Timothy David Martyn Cox (aka Son-Of-God) and charged him with nine offenses, all dealing with the possession and distribution of indecent images of children. Cox, who had been one of the pedophiles involved in Project Wickerman, saw there was a "gap in the market" and was responsible for moving the chat room somewhere else.

In fact, Cox operated the chat room out of his bedroom. Although he lived with his parents, who owned a microbrewery on the property, none of his family knew about his online activities.

When Cox was arrested, he had nearly 76,000 pornographic images of children on his computer, plus enough evidence to convict him of his online dealings by offering nearly 11,500 images to chat room users.

Nabbing Cox was a big coup, but the undercover officers on the case wanted to keep members of the chat room from getting suspicious. The officers pretended to be Cox and posted a message that he was stepping away for a 30-minute tea break. The ploy worked. The 70-plus members simply waited until Cox returned to download and view images and videos. For the next 10 days, authorities continued to operate the chat room, making more arrests, and then finally shut it down. But shutting down the second website didn't stop members from once again moving their resources and sharing the child pornography elsewhere.

Within days, Brit Gordon Mackintosh, 33 (aka "lust4skoolgurls" and "silentblackheart"), rekindled the activities in another chat room, and officials amassed more evidence and waited. By January 2007, Mackintosh was arrested on 27 counts of creating, possessing, and distributing indecent images and videos. When authorities linked more than 5,000 indecent and explicit images of children and 392 obscene movie files to him, Mackintosh pled guilty to all counts. He remains in a British jail without a scheduled hearing for his sentencing.

In addition to catching Cox and Mackintosh, law enforcement officials in 35 countries arrested more than 700 people, 200 of them in Great Britain alone. In the sting, British authorities rescued more than 30 children, ranging in age from a few months to those in their teens.

On June 18, 2007, Cox pled guilty in Britain to the nine offenses of possessing or distributing obscene photos of children and was sentenced to an indefinite jail term at Ipswich Crown Court, Buxhall, England. The court's definition of "indefinite" means that Cox will stay in prison until authorities decide that he no longer poses a threat to minors (Cox actually giggled when told he may never leave prison).

"You are obsessed with images of children being sexually abused," Judge Peter Thompson told Cox during the sentencing. "These are shocking images which involve very young children—in the worst cases being subjected to sadistic, painful abuse which you, for some distorted reason, appear to take enjoyment from." The judge said that since Cox posed "significant risks," he had to be imprisoned for public protection.

For CEOP's Gamble, the verdict represented a powerful warning for anyone using the internet to assist in sexually exploiting children.

"From the apparent 'safety' of his home, Cox spent hours each day planning, promoting, and encouraging the abuse and exploitation of innocent young victims," said Gamble. "In doing so he provided a service to hundreds of like minded individuals, enabling those with a sexual interest in children to share indecent images and discuss further plans for abuse. Any individual who thinks they can carry out such horrific activities undetected is in for a very rude awakening. The belief that the internet provides anonymity is unfounded and for Cox and Mackintosh it has already proved to be a costly misconception."

The U.S. Department of Justice (DOJ) reported that the "technological ease, lack of expense, and anonymity in obtaining and distributing child pornography (online) has resulted in an explosion in the availability, accessibility, and volume of child pornography." The DOJ estimates that 200 new pornographic images of children are posted daily to the internet's collection of more than 1 million images.

The Internet Watch Foundation website notes that "the severity of online child abuse content is increasing, with a four-fold rise in images depicting the most severe abuse, such as penetrative and sadistic sexual activity. This trend reflects an apparent growing demand for purchasing more severe images with nearly 60 percent of commercial child abuse websites selling child rape images."

In November 2006, Australian authorities discovered another online network of child pornography and engaged the help of authorities in Great Britain, the U.S., Germany, and Canada to apprehend members of the network. Authorities managed to break through the many layers of encryption, background checks, and other security measures before being approved by the site's owners. Their results provided enough evidence to convict the players and stop the child pornography ring, especially the men who preyed on its victims.

"All I can say is that they are worth the download," wrote James Freeman, 47, known in the global porn ring as "Mystikal," according to court documents. "My thanks to you and all the others that together make this the greatest group of pedos ever to gather in one place." Freeman was one of 12 Americans arrested in the sting in 11 states:

California, Connecticut, Florida, Idaho, Indiana, North Carolina, Oregon, Pennsylvania, Texas, Virginia, and Washington.

Following a 6-day trial in January 2009, Freeman was found guilty on six counts, including engaging in a child exploitation enterprise; conspiracy to advertise, transport, ship, receive, and possess child pornography; advertising, transporting, and receiving child pornography; and obstruction of justice. On April 28, he was sentenced to life in prison.

A 35-count indictment unsealed in March 2008 in the Pensacola, Florida, U.S. District Court detailed conversations among the 12 Americans accused of trading and advertising the pornography.

According to one such conversation, "This one may offend here, so a word of caution, these girls are heavily drugged," wrote 54-year-old Raymond Roy, known as "Nimo," on July 10, 2007. "Not much action to speak of, the girls are to [*sic*] (expletive deleted) up to move, or resist. Three girls, the first one being the youngest, around 8 or 9 [years old]."

Roy was sentenced to 360 months in prison on December 29, 2008, after pleading guilty to five charges, including engaging in a child exploitation enterprise; conspiracy to advertise, transport, ship, receive, and possess child pornography; advertising child pornography; transporting child pornography; and receiving child pornography.

In March 2008, 10 other men were arrested, and more than 400,000 photos, video files, and other images were confiscated, showing children as young as 5 years old engaging in sexual acts. The 10 received prison sentences ranging from 164 to 365 months.

After the arrests, J. Stephen Tidwell, FBI executive assistant director, said, "This is beyond a quantum exponential leap for us to see folks that have gone to this much trouble to produce this kind of volume of horrific exploitation of children."

While Tidwell said that 20 of the children depicted in the images had been rescued, the job for law enforcement was far from over. "But with 400,000 [images] we're going to be at this for years, trying to find the [other] victims," he said.

A year later, on March 10, 2009, the DOJ issued a press release, which in part stated: "According to a 40-count superseding indictment handed up on March 19, 2008, the defendants were members of a highly sophisticated international network. The group was a well-organized criminal enterprise whose purpose was to propagate child sex abuse images to its membership during a 2-year period. According to their plea agreements, members of the illegal organization used internet newsgroups—large file-sharing networks where text, software, pictures and videos can be traded and shared—to traffic in illegal images and videos depicting prepubescent children, including toddlers, engaged in various sexual and sadistic acts. Specifically, an Australian constable who infiltrated the group in August 2006 testified about how group members employed a complex system of pseudonyms, screening tests for new members, and sophisticated encryption methods to avoid detection. He also testified that the group traded more than 400,000 images and 1,000 videos of child sexual abuse before it was dismantled by law enforcement."

Today, law enforcement agencies worldwide are actively pursuing online pedophiles and predators in an effort to keep the world's children safe from harm. When law enforcement agencies from different countries collaborate, it represents a victory for all.

Timothy David Martyn Cox, aka Son-Of-God, who ran a website of online child pornography [Courtesy of Paul Krawczyk, Child Exploitation Section of the Toronto Police Service]

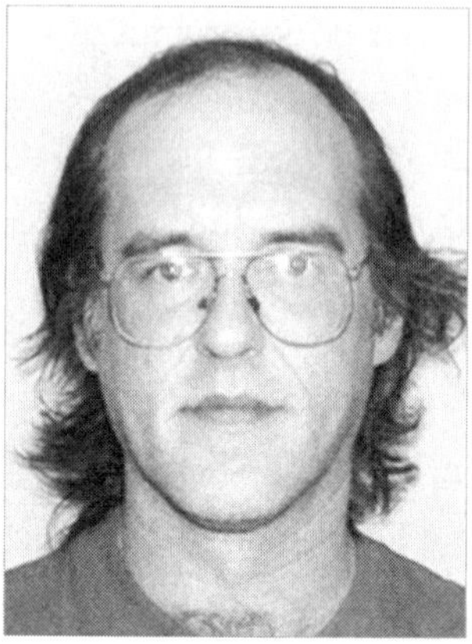

James Freeman, convicted in an international sting of online sex offenders [Courtesy of Santa Rosa Sheriff's Office]

8

Guess Who's for Dinner?

In December 2002, Armin Meiwes placed an ad on the internet. It wasn't your ordinary ad. This one was special. Meiwes was in search of someone to eat. Yes, some*one*.

A college student who saw the ad followed the links that Meiwes had previously posted about killing and cannibalizing 43-year-old Bernd Jürgen Brandes of Berlin, Germany, and called the police. After the local police read the postings and investigated the allegations, Meiwes was arrested in that same month at his home, and investigators discovered the slaughter room, body parts, and videos.

Meiwes didn't put up a fight; he admitted to what he had done. "I had the fantasy, and, in the end, I fulfilled it," he told police.

Once the media picked up the sensational story, Meiwes's neighbors were shocked. They knew him as a quiet, single man who never had wild parties. He repaired computers for a living and fixed classic vehicles in his spare time. He always smiled and waved to his neighbors.

But Meiwes had a dark side. He placed his first ad, which was short and succinct, on several websites in 2001: "Seeking young, well-built men aged 18 to 30 to slaughter."

Another, which he posted 80 times in The Cannibal Café and other chat rooms, read as follows: "Looking for a well-built man, 18–30, who would like to get eaten by me."

Out of the sea of cyberreaders, Bernd responded, "I'm your meat."

Meiwes liked the response and contacted the person who had expressed interest in becoming his next meal. As it turned out, Bernd, who undoubtedly had a death wish, was delighted. Not only was he going to be slaughtered, according to the ad, but he would also be eaten by another human. While Bernd was a bit older than Meiwes's ad had specified, Meiwes knew he was the one.

At the time, Meiwes had already responded to 203 people who had emailed him, claiming that they wanted to be "eaten." But when they saw the photos of the slaughter room he'd built in his house—showing the mattresses he'd added to soundproof the room and an old metal patio table for the butchering that would allow blood to drain to the floor—most never wrote back.

A few of Meiwes's respondents, however, did visit him at his home, with some even agreeing to let him hang them up like sides of beef. Meiwes would go so far as to mark their bodies with a pen to indicate the various cuts. None of these hardy souls ever returned, until Bernd came along.

Bernd worked in Berlin for Siemens, a major computer manufacturer, where he was well-liked by his colleagues. He was athletic and openly bisexual, and lived with another man.

Meiwes and Bernd had dark secrets they kept from those closest to them. Meiwes fantasized about killing and cannibalism. He used to videotape himself dismembering Barbie dolls and smearing himself with ketchup. When authorities confiscated his computer after his arrest, they discovered a photo of Bernd's body hanging on a meat hook with pieces of flesh ripped from it, videos of Bernd dying, and a collection of pornographic images.

Bernd's obsession with self-mutilation had turned from fantasy to a desire he needed to act on. He frequently visited a male prostitute named Emmanuel, who testified in court that Bernd had not only been getting more demanding about sex, but had begun asking Emmanuel to bite or cut off his penis. Emmanuel thought he was just joking.

"Once, I brought a knife to him during sex and told him I was going to cut it off, but I thought it was fantasy," Emmanuel said. Bernd eventually went in search of someone who would actually do it.

On March 9, 2001, Bernd boarded the train to Kassel, Germany, where Meiwes said he would meet him and take him to his gingerbread-style house in a quiet neighborhood in Rotenberg, about 90 minutes away.

Meiwes set up a video camera to film the event. In the videotape, the two men initially joked about the shadows on the slaughter room walls. Then, Bernd asked Meiwes to bite off his penis. Although Bernd's testicles burst when Meiwes began biting, his penis would not come off, so Meiwes severed it with a knife. Bernd tried to eat his own penis but complained that it was "too chewy."

Then, in true Hannibal Lecter–style, Meiwes sautéed the penis in a pan with salt, pepper, wine, and garlic, plus some fat that he had already cut from Bernd's torso. But the penis burned, so Meiwes cut it up and put it in the dog dish. While Meiwes was busy cooking, Bernd lay in a bathtub bleeding and unconscious from the alcohol, painkillers, and sleeping pills Meiwes had given him.

For the next 3 hours, Meiwes read a *Star Trek* novel and waited for Bernd to die. When he felt the process was taking too long, he finally killed Bernd by stabbing him in the throat. Meiwes then hung Bernd's body on a meat hook and began tearing chunks of flesh from the body with his hands. He didn't want to waste any parts, so he even ground up the bones into powder to use as flour.

Over the next few months, Meiwes savored every meal he made with parts of Bernd. He ate some of Bernd's remains with eggs for breakfast or for lunch. He was convinced that the more he ate, the closer he was to his victim. He confided to a reporter from *Stern*, the German newsmagazine, that his English became better with each meal due to Bernd's excellent command of the language.

Later, at the trial, Meiwes bragged that he drank a robust South African red wine the first time he ate Bernd's flesh, which he said tasted much like pork.

In court, two psychiatrists testified that Meiwes and Bernd had both had very bad relationships with their mothers. Meiwes's mother was described as a domineering woman who berated her son in public; she accompanied him on dates and army outings, and lived with him until she died. As a defense mechanism, Meiwes invented and talked to an imaginary brother named Franky. He would use the name later when posting online and joining chat rooms.

Likewise, Bernd shouldered tremendous guilt, blaming himself for his mother's death in a car accident when he was 12, although his father told him she had committed suicide.

Meiwes's defense attorney referred to the crime as a case of assisted suicide and not murder. He claimed that cannibalism was not illegal in Germany and asserted that the victim willingly allowed himself to be killed. Assisted suicide carries a 5-year maximum sentence.

Prosecutors challenged the defense by pursuing a conviction for "murder for sexual satisfaction" and "disturbing the peace of the dead."

On January 30, 2004, after Meiwes was found guilty of manslaughter and sentenced to 8 years and 6 months in prison, he admitted to what he had done in a *Welt am Sonntag* newspaper article. "I accept that I am guilty and I regret my actions."

But the ordeal was far from over. Prosecutors appealed the sentence, claiming that Meiwes should have been convicted of murder. At the retrial in April 2005, a psychologist noted that Meiwes still "had fantasies about devouring the flesh of young people" and could kill again.

When the trial finally ended on May 10, 2006, Meiwes was found guilty of murder and sentenced to life in prison. He has reportedly said he wants to write a book about his life in the hope that it will prevent others from doing what he did.

"They should go for treatment, so it doesn't escalate like it did with me," said Meiwes.

Forensic expert Manfred Risse, who worked on this case, did write a book in 2007 titled *Last Supper of the Murderers*. Also, a movie based on this gruesome tale was released in 2005, appropriately titled *Cannibal*.

***

Fantasies about cannibalism that flourish on the internet still become a reality for some. Take Kevin Ray Underwood of Purcell, Oklahoma. Underwood was obsessed with the movie *Silence of the*

Lambs. He regarded the main character, Hannibal Lecter, as his hero and wrote on his Myspace profile about his own cannibalistic fantasies: "If you were a cannibal, what would you wear to dinner?" He answered his own question with, "The skin of last night's main course."

He described himself online as a "single, bored and lonely" man with "dangerously weird" fantasies. When he wasn't restocking shelves at the grocery store where he worked, he stayed home with his pet rat, browsing the internet, posting entries on his blogs, and playing the computer role-playing game Kingdom of Loathing. On February 4, 2006, he posted a rambling note on his blog:

> I've been really bad again lately. I need to have the doctor write me a prescription for more Lexapro or something, and start taking that again. I wonder if they even still make Lexapro? I checked some of those online pharmacies, to see if I could get it cheaper from Canada or something, but none of them I've looked at have it. They have five or six other antidepressants and anti-anxiety medications, but not that one.

On April 12, 2006, the 28-year-old Underwood did the unthinkable. He lured his 10-year-old neighbor, Jamie Rose Bolen, into his apartment, hit her in the head with a cutting board, and then suffocated her.

The day after the murder, he wrote online, "I've been nervous all day. I'm afraid the cops would come into my apartment and see all the knives and swords and horror movies and commentaries about serial killers on my DVD rack and suspect me."

While police were investigating Jamie's disappearance as a possible kidnapping, they had set up a roadblock at an intersection near the apartment building. Underwood was in one of the cars they stopped, and the officers remembered him as being a bit odd. They talked to him, but let him go. By 4:00 PM that afternoon, the police were suspicious enough to knock on Underwood's apartment door.

"Go ahead and arrest me. She is in there. I chopped her up," he told them. Police found Jamie's body stuffed into a plastic storage tub sealed with duct tape in the bedroom closet. She had been nearly decapitated and had knife marks elsewhere on her neck; she had also been sexually assaulted.

The police confiscated the arsenal of weapons he had mentioned online, along with meat tenderizers, barbecue skewers, and sex toys. Although he did not appear to have cannibalized anyone, police found plenty of evidence to indicate that he had plans to do so sooner or later.

"This appears to have been part of a plan to kidnap a person, rape them, torture them, kill them, cut off their head, drain the body of blood, rape the corpse, then dispose of the organs and bones," said David Tomkins, Purcell's chief of police.

In March 2008, as the jury trial was in progress, district attorney Greg Mashburn showed graphic photos of the crime scene and played Underwood's videotaped confession that provided details about his fantasies of cannibalism, torture, and murder. The district attorney was seeking the death penalty.

"This was the worst of the worst," Mashburn told the jury. "There are cases for life without parole and for the possibility of parole. This just isn't it. He should forfeit his life because this was so bad."

The defense team claimed that Underwood's depression and a personality disorder were to blame for his crimes, but the prosecutors didn't believe it.

"Even if he was depressed, what does that do?" Mashburn asked. "Does that give him a green light to butcher a little girl?"

On April 3, 2008, the jury took less than an hour to find Underwood guilty of first degree murder, and he was sentenced to death by lethal injection. Although he remains in jail, he appealed his sentence in October 2010. His appeal was denied.

***

In yet another recent cannibalism case, Karina Barduchian, a 16-year-old Russian girl, disappeared on her way to school in St. Petersburg, Russia, on January 19, 2009. Two 19-year-old men, Maxim Golovatskikh, a butcher, and Yuri Mozhnov, a florist, were charged with her murder. Authorities said the two men kidnapped the girl, drowned her in a bathtub, and cut her body into pieces.

Sergei Kapitonov, a spokesman for St. Petersburg's prosecutors, testified, "They said they ate the girl's body parts because they were hungry." He claimed they baked her organs in an oven and ate them with potatoes. The two were apprehended when plastic bags containing some of the girl's body parts were found and traced back to the pair.

Karina's friend Ekaterina Zinovyeva later testified at the trial that she and Karina had gone to Golovatskikh's apartment to party with him and Mozhnov. Karina had a crush on Mozhnov and stayed the night with him, while Zinovyeva went to sleep in another room.

"I was sleepy but heard splashes of water and some noise there but was not worried," Zinovyeva said. "Sometime later I woke up and decided to check what was going on. I went to the bathroom but Yury [*sic*] stopped me on the way and told me to go back to bed. They had joked earlier that they could kill Karina but, of course, I couldn't believe for a second that they were serious."

During the final stage of trial, Karina's relatives and witnesses received anonymous threats via the internet a few days before the verdict was announced, according to reports in the *Komsomolskaya Pravda* daily. One of Karina's friends had been worried that she would end up suffering the same fate as Karina if she testified. A profile was opened on the VKontakte social networking site (similar to Facebook) in Karina's name and featured a photo of a disfigured female face.

On May 5, 2010, Golovatskikh was sentenced to 19 years in prison; Mozhnov was sentenced to 18 years. They are each required to pay Karina's family almost $40,000 in compensation.

Karina's mother, Nadya Barduchian, 45, shared her grief at the sentencing: "Our lives are ruined by Karina's death and the horrible way she died," she said. "[The killers] showed no remorse. They were oblivious to the pain they'd caused. They were so calm and matter of fact as they told how they'd killed and cooked her. I still don't understand why they did it."

Jamie Rose Bolen, killed by her neighbor Kevin Ray Underwood [Courtesy of Bonnie Kernene, mylifeofcrime.wordpress.com]

Underwood after his arrest and before his eventual sentence of death [Courtesy of Purcell Police Department]

9

The First Internet Serial Killer

"I'm your slave. I'm yours." A dark-haired woman named Suzette Trouten looked directly into the video camera as she pledged her undying devotion to a 58-year-old man known as the "Slavemaster." She sat on the edge of the motel bed and waited for the videotape to stop and the action to begin.

John Robinson just smiled.

By day, middle-aged Robinson led a seemingly normal life. Neighbors called him a wonderful guy who gardened and entertained his grandchildren; he seemed to be happily married, too. But by night, Robinson—aka the Slavemaster—had a dark side as a well-known master of a troupe of sex slaves, most of whom he first met online.

Robinson trolled the internet hunting for new victims, although he says his killing spree started long before the internet was created. He won't admit to how many women he killed, but police can link him to the murders of least five.

Between 1969 and 2000, Robinson spent some 15 years off and on in prison for an assortment of theft and fraud charges. During the time that he was serving one of his sentences between 1987 and 1993, he met and wooed prison librarian Beverly Bonner. Robinson convinced Beverly that he was in love with her, and they decided to get married after Robinson was released. Robinson started using the alias of James Turner after he left prison, and he and Beverly moved to Olathe, Kansas, after she divorced her husband. Beverly started working for Robinson, who was then president of HydroGro, Inc. No one ever heard from her again.

Beverly had told her ex-husband and friends that she was traveling abroad on business with Robinson and gave them a post office box for her mail. Her ex-husband sent the alimony checks there on a regular basis, and Robinson routinely cashed the checks, so no one was ever suspicious. When Robinson tired of Beverly, he made sure she disappeared without a trace. He rented a storage unit and moved her belongings into it. Among the items that he tucked into the storage unit was the 55-gallon chemical drum that held Beverly's body, along with two other similar drums containing the bodies of two other women. The other two women had been receiving government checks, which Robinson continued to cash for pocket money.

Robinson managed to keep his double life a secret for years, even from his wife, Nancy, to whom he'd been married since 1964. While Nancy managed the mobile home park where they lived, Robinson had launched his own venture: a magazine about mobile home living that became relatively successful. Robinson's employment options were somewhat compromised by his prior criminal record, so Nancy was pleased that her husband had found interesting work to keep him busy. Little did she know that he had become the Slavemaster in his off hours.

Robinson kept a regular daily routine. He waited for Nancy to leave for the office and then browsed various chat rooms online to find women who were interested in BDSM—an acronym combining the terms *bondage* and *discipline*, *dominance* and *submission*, and *sadism* and *masochism*. He often posted online about his ideal woman: submissive and willing to engage in virtually any imaginable sex act. When the internet and chat rooms were no longer enough to satisfy his deviant needs, he combed through the classifieds in alternative newspapers for local women who were looking for rough sex.

The women Robinson met online were easily seduced by his charming prose, and he shared photographs of himself with a select few. Some agreed to meet him in person in Kansas City, Kansas, on an all-expenses-paid trip to do his bidding, no matter how perverse his sexual request. It was a wild but brief rendezvous for some; for others, it would end in death.

In late 1997, Robinson met Izabela Lewicka, a 21-year-old Polish college student living in north central Indiana with her university professor parents. Izabela wrote online about her interest in gothic horror stories and bondage, which intrigued Robinson so much that he offered her an "internship" as his slave. She accepted his invitation and told her parents she was dropping out of college and moving to Kansas City, fabricating a story about a rich publisher who had offered her an opportunity she couldn't refuse.

When Robinson met Izabela in Kansas City, he dazzled her with an engagement ring, whisked her off to the county registrar's office, and paid for a marriage certificate that he never picked up. Izabela assumed they were legally married, and she signed a 115-page slave contract that gave Robinson control over her life, including access to her bank accounts. From that point on, she communicated with her parents only via email.

Less than 2 years later, Robinson told friends that he and Izabela were going on a long trip. After the couple left Kansas City, no one ever saw her again.

Even before Izabela's disappearance, Robinson had been trolling chat rooms and websites in search of a replacement sex slave. He soon found the perfect woman. Like Robinson, 28-year-old Suzette led a double life. By day, she was a caring, licensed practical nurse; by night, she submitted to a host of masters as a sex slave.

Suzette was lured into Robinson's trap when he told her online that he was a wealthy businessman who needed a full-time nurse for his elderly father. He promised her a salary of $60,000 per year, plus a series of all-expenses-paid trips around the world for the three of them. And, of course, she would agree to be his slave.

Suzette told her family and friends that she had accepted "a dream job." When she moved to Kansas City in February 1999, she left Robinson's name and telephone number with her mother in case of emergency. In her last email to a friend, Suzette wrote, "We all finally find what we want and need and I found mine."

Suzette's mother received several typed letters from her daughter by post, but something wasn't right. Suzette didn't spell well, yet the spelling and grammar in the letters was flawless. The envelopes carried postmarks from Kansas City rather than the foreign destinations she had described. Deeply concerned, Suzette's mother called one of the emergency phone numbers her daughter had given her. When Robinson answered the phone, she asked to speak to her daughter, but Robinson refused, insisting that Suzette had stolen money from him and run off with one of his friends. He cut the conversation short by hanging up the phone.

Highly suspicious of Robinson, Suzette's mother called the police to file a missing person's report. When one of the officers recognized Robinson's name from previous missing persons inquiries, the authorities stepped up their investigation, hoping for the break they needed to catch a serial killer.

Unaware of the investigation, Robinson soon returned to his BDSM chat rooms. He even posed as Suzette when members expressed curiosity over her sudden disappearance. When some members began asking tough questions, Robinson stopped posing as Suzette, instead posting as the Slavemaster and another persona he called "JA Robinson." Some of Suzette's friends decided to check out the Slavemaster and took turns chatting with him. Once again, Robinson appeared to have his pick of willing slaves. He set his sights on Lore Remington, a young woman living in eastern Canada.

Lore told Robinson she was very interested in becoming his slave. The chat room messages progressed to emails and then to phone calls. The Lenaxa, Kansas, police department had previously tapped Robinson's phone as part of the ongoing investigation. Authorities took a gamble and contacted Lore to let her know about the investigation and asked if she would help with the case. She agreed.

Although Lore tried to get Robinson to make overt promises or admit guilt about his past dealings with women, his responses remained guarded. As she recalled, he "offered nothing other than that I would be financially taken care of and never have to work." Lore hedged, telling Robinson she didn't seem to be his kind of slave.

Neither would commit to taking the next step, so the relationship went no further.

Robinson soon met a woman named Vickie Neufeld in one of the chat rooms he frequented. Vickie had just been laid off from her job and was depressed, making her a perfect target. Robinson's many emails and phone calls convinced her that his many connections would help her find a good job. Of course, part of the deal was that she would become his slave. She didn't want to move from Texas to Kansas City, but he offered to take care of all of her expenses and assured her that she could pay him back when she found a job. The police, who were monitoring Robinson's calls by this time, were certain the Slavemaster was circling his next victim.

Robinson wired money to Vickie, who came to Kansas City armed with more than $700 worth of sex toys and BDSM accessories. Robinson reserved a motel room and prepared for a night of rough sex with Vickie. As the police monitored the encounter from the next room, Vickie complained that Robinson's demands as a master were too much for her. He didn't like her attitude. He tied her up, beat her, and took photos of her in compromising positions. When the physical abuse finally ended, he left her tied up and alone in the motel room for a few days. The police did not intervene, just in case Robinson returned or if he was watching to see if she escaped. When Robinson did return, he told her to go back to Texas and wait for further orders. As his slave, she left obediently in keeping with his wishes, and he kept her collection of sex toys.

This became a pattern that Robinson repeated with several women. He brought them to the same motel, had rough sex with them, assaulted them, took photos of the bruises and marks on their bodies, and then left them alone in the room for a few days to think about their roles as slaves. When he returned, he would send them home to await his further orders.

A woman named Jeanna Milliron would turn out to be more resourceful than the rest. As usual, Robinson ordered her to come to Kansas City, and she followed his demands. He assaulted her and abandoned her in the motel, as he had done with the others, but

Jeanna found a way to free herself from Robinson's bondage and called the police.

Now that a credible witness had come forward, county prosecutor Paul Morrison agreed to issue a warrant for Robinson's arrest, but concerns remained. Issuing a warrant for sexual battery was one thing, but in order to prosecute Robinson for the unsolved murders, the prosecutor needed more evidence—ideally, another victim he could tie the Slavemaster to.

New evidence was produced through the police phone tap on Robinson. He was communicating with a woman in Tennessee about her plans to move to Kansas City to become his latest slave; police were alarmed to discover that she planned to bring her 8-year-old daughter with her. Combing through the list of women Robinson was known to have brought to the motel, police located Vickie in Texas; they were able to convince her to file a complaint against Robinson for sexual battery and theft.

In June 2000, authorities arrived at Robinson's mobile home and arrested him. The police not only had search warrants for his mobile home but for a ranch he owned about 30 miles away. Robinson didn't believe the police had any incriminating evidence against him, as he was unaware of the phone taps and ongoing surveillance.

Robinson's "ranch" was no more than an old, deserted mobile home and a dilapidated barn on the edge of a large pond overrun by tall grass. The Kansas Bureau of Investigation brought in cadaver-sniffing dogs and began to inspect every inch of the property.

On one side of the barn, two 55-gallon yellow chemical drums were barely visible among the tall weeds. After darting around the barn briefly, the cadaver-sniffing dogs sat down in front of the drums and refused to move.

"It was horrendous," Sgt. Rick Roth testified at the trial, recalling that when they took the lid off the first drum, the smell of decaying flesh made investigators gag. Inside the drum was the body of a young woman partially submerged in fluid. The police didn't bother opening the second drum; they already knew what it contained. Both drums were taken to the county morgue, where officials found the badly decomposed body of a second woman. The remains were eventually identified as those of Izabela and Suzette.

Just over the state line in Missouri, police obtained a search warrant for the storage facility where Robinson had rented two units. They found three more chemical drums inside, all containing bodies in various stages of decomposition. One victim was identified as Beverly; the two others were women who had been reported missing after telling family and friends they were going to work for Robinson in Kansas City.

Autopsies later revealed that all five women had died quickly from blunt-force trauma to the head. The report offered their families some relief; at least the women hadn't suffered long. But authorities knew these were all premeditated killings.

Police obtained a third search warrant to gain access to the apartment that Robinson had rented for Izabela. The landlord told authorities that while most of the apartment had been dusty and unkempt when Robinson left with Izabela's furniture and belongings, the bedroom looked like it had been cleaned and repainted. Authorities sprayed Luminol—a blood-detecting chemical that glows under ultraviolet light—on the bedroom walls and floor and found traces of blood.

Although police didn't uncover any additional bodies at the time, incriminating evidence was found linking Robinson to two other missing women. The county prosecutor in Kansas City charged Robinson with theft and sexual battery against his motel victims as well as three counts of murder (of Suzette, Izabela, and Lisa Stasi, a third victim). Missouri prosecutors added three more capital murder charges to Robinson's list of crimes. He was held on a $5 million bond in maximum security.

Robinson's Kansas trial took place in October 2002. His public defender, Byron Cerillo, chastised the media for sensationalizing the trial, saying, "I resent the fact that people are now claiming that Mr. Robinson, either directly or indirectly, is a serial killer."

Robinson's family released a statement that read, in part, "As each day has passed, the surreal events have built into a narrative that is almost beyond comprehension. While we do not discount the information that has and continues to come to light, we do not know the person whom we have read and heard about on TV. The John Robinson we know has always been a loving and caring father."

During the trial, the evidence included the infamous 40-minute video of Robinson and Beverly having sadomasochistic sex in a motel room, which the jury was required to watch. Most of them covered their eyes during parts of the video.

Early in the video, Beverly said, "This is what you wanted me to tell you. I'm your slave … Everything is yours."

Robinson responded by telling her, "The most important thing in life is you are my slave."

More than 100 witnesses testified for the prosecution during the 3-week trial. The jury deliberated quickly, finding Robinson guilty on three counts of murder. In January 2003, judge John Anderson III sentenced Robinson to death for each count of murder, plus a life sentence.

The state of Missouri also wanted to try Robinson for three murders, but the defendant knew Missouri judges were much more favorable to death penalty sentences than their Kansas counterparts and he fought to postpone extradition for the Missouri trial. After a seemingly endless round of negotiations between his lawyers and Missouri prosecutors, the parties agreed to accept guilty pleas for the murders in exchange for life without parole.

Robinson's wife Nancy filed for divorce in February 2005. But because there was no follow-through by either party, the divorce was never granted.

In July 2009, Robinson appealed his conviction, claiming he had not received a fair trial. Paige Nichols, his attorney, said Nancy had been coerced into cooperating with officials by hinting that she had helped Robinson commit the murders.

"That attitude pervaded this case, led to multiple illegal searches, and resulted in rushed pretrial proceedings and a patently unfair trial," Nichols wrote in the appeal.

Nichols also claimed that the judge who issued the search warrant leading to the discovery of Suzette's and Izabela's bodies did not have jurisdiction.

That appeal was denied, and Robinson remains on death row at the El Dorado Correctional Facility in Kansas.

Suzette Trouten, murdered by serial killer John Robinson [Courtesy of Lenexa Police Department]

Beverly Bonner, Robinson's apparent first victim [Courtesy of Lenexa Police Department]

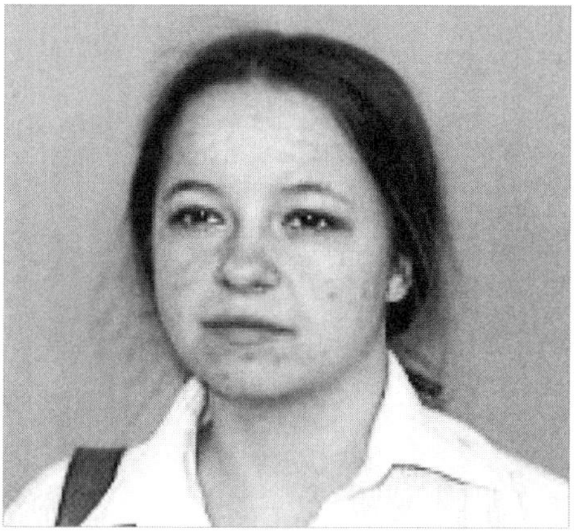

Izabela Lewicka, a Polish student killed by Robinson [Courtesy of Lenexa Police Department]

Robinson after many years spent in prison [Courtesy of Lenexa Police Department]

10

Swedish Phishing

"PLEASE leave me ALONE!" Angry, frustrated, and fearful, Melissa frantically typed the email message and hit the Send button.

How much more could she take? The harassing emails from a man she had met only once had continued for 11 long years, and still there seemed to be no end in sight. When it started she was in high school; now she was married and pregnant with her second child. Given the most recent messages, she decided that her cyberstalker wasn't just a harmless nut. He was going to do something crazy.

It all began in 1999, when Melissa's sister, Veronica, went out on a date with Martin Amsteus, a Swedish citizen who was visiting the U.S. The two dined at the restaurant where Melissa was working as a waitress at the time, and for reasons she cannot fathom to this day, Amsteus left the restaurant convinced that one of the sisters had fallen in love with him. From his home in Sweden, he began sending strange, unwanted email messages to Melissa. She cancelled her email account and signed up with a new service, but he soon tracked her down and resumed writing her.

At times, there would be a lull in Amsteus's email campaign, and Melissa would breathe a sigh of relief. But he would always reappear. On Valentine's Day 2008, her sister-in-law Rikki received flowers at her home in North Carolina. Although Rikki first assumed they were from her husband, Marcus, the card was from a man she'd never met—Amsteus. In it, he begged her to send him contact information for Melissa and Veronica.

Rikki ignored Amsteus, but he had discovered her email address and began writing her. Not wanting to alarm her husband or his sisters, Rikki kept Amsteus's communications secret at first, but as the messages grew increasingly acrimonious, she confided to Marcus about the situation. He emailed Amsteus, asking him to leave his wife alone, at which point the sulking Swede began directing his tirades at Marcus.

"He apparently had chatted with my sisters online over 10 years previously," Marcus said. "At this time they must have been 17 or 18 years old. I knew nothing of it, but I'm sure they just decided to grow up like everyone else and cut off their ties to online chatting. Either that or this guy started really freaking them out so they banished him."

For 2 weeks, Marcus emailed Amsteus telling him he would not provide any information about his sisters. But Amsteus was desperate and determined to find out why Melissa and Veronica had stopped replying to his messages. He'd called Melissa at one point, Marcus learned, but she'd told him there was nothing between them and that he should stop contacting her.

"Mind you, this was over 10 years ago, and apparently my sisters were still avoiding him," Marcus said. "He kept wanting me to give him my dad's email address 'because he can solve this.' I refused and told him nothing good could come of this. He was threatening to come over here, and I honestly was not sure if he was the most sane person."

By May 2008, Amsteus was sending more than a dozen emails a day to Marcus at his office at a North Carolina college. The messages were often shrill diatribes such as this one:

> And Marcus, what about that they would tell you who Veronica called that night, because you are Veronica's brother and she would tell you—how come I still don't KNOW, what kind if a sick game are you playing, why do you allow it to ruin somebody's life.
>
> If you do not answer/give me David's [the father's] email address, I will write others at your school explaining this in detail and asking

> them to ask you. I have no other choice. I have to solve this. Believe me, I am not trying to be mean. How long have I waited to get this solved ... how much time of my life have I lost, what are the alternatives, what options do I have, this will just continue otherwise. I don't know what happened, I don't know who I talked to. Melissa refuses to answer even what clearly pertains to her. I rest my case. Your choice, give me Davids email address, please, or have other people around you sent a detailed explaination of this and the request to ask you to give it to me.

At other times, the emails arrived with only subject lines and no text in the body:

> Subject: I want to solve what happened that is All, is that strange or hard?
>
> Subject: You choose how long this will go on. It is THAT simple.
>
> Subject: If it bothers you that I write, I will go over there, will write physical letters, WHY not give me ...

That same month, Marcus sought help from WHOA, the online safety organization. WHOA sent official complaints to Amsteus's ISP as well as to Yahoo! and Hotmail, where he had email accounts. Yahoo! quickly responded, saying that it had "taken appropriate action against the Yahoo! accounts in question, as per our Terms of Service (TOS)," but it would not disclose "the action taken on another user's account with a third party."

Hotmail followed suit, but there was no response from Telia, Amsteus's ISP in Sweden. For several weeks the emails stopped, but it would not be for long.

On May 27, Rikki received a series of rambling messages from Amsteus, which she refused to answer. Telia had notified him about WHOA's complaint, and he complained to Melissa:

> Look, this is most likely going to court now anyway, because Rikki sent a complain to that

> organization who contacted Telia who is my internet provider, and she obviously claimed that I was threatening her. This information Telia relayed to me, which means that I report them to datainspektionen, since they cannot, according to Swedish law keep that kind of information on me. Telia sent me a letter about this, and I have asked them to send me a copy on all information they have and letting then know that all of it goes to datainspektionen. Also, to claim that I threathened anybody is slander, which is a crime. All this will go, together with a description of this from the beginning to the end to that organisation too, I can't remember the name of it. Get it? So I am going straight to Church street to hand this over in writing and then we can meet in court. I cannot be the only one trying. If you don't want me to even try I wont, which means I will hand this over everything, from the beginning, in writing to David instead, and then you may as well give me his [David's] email address."

When Marcus learned that Amsteus was continuing to email Melissa, he asked her to forward everything to WHOA. He was growing more and more concerned about the bizarre messages the Swede was sending family members, including this one to Melissa:

> To say that I threathened her is low. I want to know how you think or feel about this, if you feel the same? Because then we are not at square 0 we are at square -1. Remember how I explained how you saing you hate me etc., made it worse to me in that it becomes more important to me to solve. That is what saying I threathened does. I have zero respect for that woman now, zero. Haven't I tried to confide and explain everything about this to you
>
> Please let me know what you think. Can we please meet somewhere, just to meet up, it would be a huge step in solving this and in me getting over it, honestly Melissa, you know that, so can we? (please) Or should I go and try to talk to Veronica first?

WHOA filed more complaints with Yahoo! and Telia. Yahoo! again quickly took action by canceling the accounts. On July 11, WHOA officials received a long-winded comment from Amsteus:

> With regard to your message to Telia, who is my internet provider, where you claim that I harass these people: This issue is now under criminal investigation. I am currently looking into the US laws on organizatons, such as yours, handling private email; over here, in Sweden, it is completely restricted by law, thus the investigation. I will also, in short, send you a full description of what this whole case is about, which includes multiple fraud. I will further provide you with evidence how this Markus says he could ask other people involved on a critical issue that would be step to completely solve this, because he is their brother, and they would listen to him, waving a carrot - but did not - when I it would take him 10 seconds and I have spent 10 years. My full description will make it obvious how your message to Telia is slander, which at least in this country is criminal.
>
> Overall: You can try to solve something with sombody, if that person refuses to listen, you can either take it to court or ask somebody nearby, to avoid taking it to court and create hassle.

Officials at WHOA were concerned that Telia had breached the confidentiality of its complaint and they sent an email advising the ISP that "cyberstalking, according to the U.S. Department of Justice is 'the use of the internet, email, or other electronic communications devices to stalk another person. Stalking generally involves harassing or threatening behavior that an individual engages in repeatedly.'"

Telia responded, defending its actions: "We do not give away names of private persons in cases that we investigate. Every user has the right to know what caused the warning that was sent to him. This case has reached an unpleasant level, that is true, but we find it hard to believe that any authority in Sweden will take his complaints seriously."

WHOA instructed Marcus and Melissa to file reports about Amsteus with their local police departments. But Amsteus wasn't finished yet. On July 12, he sent another rambling message to WHOA, which read, in part:

> Below you will find a short description. Look, this started 10 years ago. And I asked for it to be solved from day one. ...
>
> I was an exchange student (the only one on campus, I think) at this small town college and this girl started talking to me over the school network, not like MSN, similar to MSN, but you saw the other one writing on real time letter by letter in real time. Now, this girl (V) is in her last year in high school, so she is using her older sister's email account at the college to access the system. You spend hours writing on this thing, so we talked and talked, talked on the phone, she asked me to go to a football game with her; we went to a restaurant where she and her sister worked.
>
> At the restaurant I meet her sister (M), the one owning the college email / chat access account; it turned out to be the one I had had a serious crush since before I started talking to V: The kind of thing where you hold eye contact a bit longer than necessary. Anyway I spend more time talking to V, and she tells me very personal things about her past ... that makes me really protective of her.
>
> We talk every night over this chat. I started to like her a lot. Then she started to say things like this has to end, I can't do this anymore for people get hurt around me and I worried my ass it and over her. I told her, the only way you can hurt me is by leaving me alone..I said so truthfully. I wrote her very very private and personal emails. ... I don't know ... part of me were maybe suspecting I was talking to more then one person by then. ... During this time I sent her some very emotional, private email. Then the same person who had said what do you not know about her was able to quote some of the very personal

> things I had written her. And it seems these emails where forwarded around campus.
>
> I have no choice but to ask them, try, beg and plead. So what do they do, they say they hate me, that what I say doesn't count, I don't matter, I am psycho, I need professional help, shout that I should leave them alone, I should grow up, they complain that I won't leave them alone, but they refuse to tell me who she called or to solve this.
>
> I have explained how much misery this creates me, how it tears me and my life apart, they know this. I have lost ten years of my life because of this; their argument is that because this much time has passed and I am not over it I am the one who is weird and therefore it should not be solved (!!) ... I will loose everything I have over this, my job, everything. For what, why? It didn't happen yesterday, I have pointed out a billion time ... not telling me what happened means that, to me, it is still going on.

Amsteus followed this with an even longer message, and WHOA filed additional complaints. When it appeared Telia had canceled Amsteus's account, he moved to an internet café in Sweden and resumed sending email to Melissa, as well as filling out comment forms on the WHOA website. WHOA continued to send complaints to Hotmail, Yahoo!, and the internet café.

On July 22, Amsteus sent Melissa another message, which in part said, "What do you need, do I have to sit outside your house and weep? What is it that is not understood?"

The following day, Melissa's nightmare came true: Amsteus appeared on her doorstep.

"He rang the doorbell ... my dog barked like crazy. When I went to see who it was ... I had no clue, so I just asked, 'May I help you?'" Melissa recalled. "Then he said he was looking for Veronica. I could tell from his accent that it was Martin. I simply told him Veronica didn't live here. Then he asked if her address was 702a or 702b. I repeated, 'She doesn't live here.'" To Melissa's great relief, he got into a car and drove off.

Melissa immediately called her husband, Brian, who was on his way home, to tell him that Amsteus had just left and was probably headed to her sister's home. Then she called Veronica to let her know what was happening. Armed with a description of the vehicle, Brian caught up with Amsteus and began to tail him. Amsteus passed Veronica's house and then turned around, apparently aware he was being followed. Brian pulled into Veronica's driveway, went into the house where his sister-in-law was sitting with her two children, and called the police.

When Amsteus knocked at the door, Veronica ignored him until the police arrived, then opened the door and told him to leave. He didn't budge until the police ordered him to go.

"You didn't have to call the police," Amsteus said to Veronica. "Nobody ever told me to leave you alone or that you didn't want to talk to me."

The police waited until Amsteus had left the neighborhood in his rental car and then put out an all-points bulletin to make sure he didn't return.

The next day, Amsteus emailed Melissa to explain his actions. She forwarded the long, drawn-out message to the police. Veronica's fiancé, Justin, sent Amsteus a reply:

> I am Veronica's fiancé. Veronica and her kids are MY FAMILY. You going to my girlfriend's house was not a good idea. Veronica doesn't want to have anything to do with you. She doesn't like you, love you, or want to be associated with you. You have upset the balance of her house and family by showing up and scaring the children. Not to mention showing up at her sister's house and scaring her.
>
> Leave her alone. Leave her family alone. If anybody in the neighborhood sees you they will call the police. There is a retired state trooper living beside Veronica and a Detective that lives across the street from her and me. I am also in law enforcement. If you continue to email, harass, or show up where Veronica is or the places she is at, then legal action will be taken. I am asking you again, man to man, adult to adult, have no further

> contact with Veronica or her family. I don't know what you think you had with Veronica. Veronica states that she was 16 when she met you and that there was never anything there. Some people in law enforcement would view this behavior from you as obsessive. I hope you read this carefully and move on.

Amsteus said he was willing to meet Justin to talk about it man to man, but Justin refused to respond. So Amsteus emailed Melissa instead and threatened to send letters to everyone in her neighborhood as well as Veronica's to tell them all about the situation.

By July 29, the police had launched an official investigation and found that Amsteus had flown from Sweden to Atlanta, rented a car, and then driven to North Carolina. They were keeping an eye on his hotel. The same day, Melissa's father received a 14-page letter via certified mail from Amsteus, which he passed on to the police. The police advised Veronica to move out of her house until Amsteus returned to Sweden. She and her children went to stay with her parents while the investigation continued.

In August 2008, Amsteus returned to Sweden, and within a month, he started to email Melissa again. Melissa refused to respond and reported the messages to the police. In what had become a predictable routine by now, every time Yahoo! and Hotmail closed one of Amsteus's email accounts, he would open a new one and continue writing Melissa.

Since early 2009, Melissa has had a new email account and only gives the address to people she knows and trusts. This has seemed to work. Until fairly recently, she was receiving the occasional Facebook message from Amsteus, which she would quickly delete, blocking him from further contact.

To the best of WHOA's knowledge, Amsteus has made no further trips to the U.S., and his emails to Melissa and her family have ceased.

One can only hope that he is out of their lives for good.

11

Virtually Bullied to Death

On January 14, 2010, 12-year-old Lauren Prince came home from school as usual and went to see what her older sister was doing. As Lauren entered her apartment building, she stopped and stared. What she saw in the hallway took her breath away: Her sister, Phoebe, still dressed in her school clothes, was hanging in the stairwell. Wrapped around Phoebe's neck was the scarf Lauren had given her for Christmas just a few weeks ago.

Six months earlier, in the summer of 2009, Phoebe Prince and her family moved to South Hadley, Massachusetts. Phoebe was now a vibrant 15-year-old with a contagious laugh and a captivating smile. Her mother, Annie O'Brien Prince, had left County Clare, Ireland, to start a new life with her family in America, bringing with her two of her daughters, Lauren and Phoebe. Annie's husband, Jeremy Prince, remained in Ireland with the couple's three other children in order to sell the house. Annie had some relatives in South Hadley, a town with a growing Irish population, and she considered the community to be a home away from home. She and Jeremy looked forward to reuniting their close-knit family as soon as possible.

Phoebe was excited when she started her freshman year at South Hadley High School in September 2009. With her striking good looks and lilting Irish accent, it didn't take her long to win the hearts of just about everyone at school, especially the boys. By December, she was dating Sean Mulveyhill, 17, a star football player and one of the most popular boys in school. Many of the girls were openly jealous of

Phoebe, and several began taunting her in the school hallways, calling her an "Irish whore." Though Phoebe did her best to take the high road and ignore the insults, it wasn't easy.

Mulveyhill and Phoebe dated for a short time before he got back together with his former girlfriend, Kayla Narey. A few weeks later, Phoebe started dating another football player, 18-year-old Austin Renaud, who was involved at the time with Flannery Mullins, age 16. Upset by all the attention Phoebe was getting, Narey and Mullins teamed up with some mutual friends to teach the new girl a lesson.

The bullying was subtle at first, but it soon escalated. Messages claiming that Phoebe was out to steal everyone's boyfriends began appearing on Facebook, along with a comment that she should just kill herself. Phoebe was roughed up in the hallways, shoved into lockers, and pushed around in the girls' restroom. As she walked to and from her classes, some of the girls whispered insults; others simply pointed an accusing finger at her without saying a word. Text messages on Phoebe's cell phone wielded more insults, and a photo of her was posted on a school wall accompanied by an obscene comment. By the time faculty removed the photo, Phoebe had already seen it and the damage was done. On one occasion, a teacher found Phoebe crying, and though she tried to talk to her, she remembers the girl as inconsolable.

Phoebe endured brutal insults, from "I hate stupid sluts" echoing in the hallway to "Why don't you just open up your legs?" shouted in the school auditorium during assembly. One girl yelled at Phoebe in the school cafeteria, calling her a "ho" and accusing her of stealing Mulveyhill away from Narey. Mulveyhill joined in, further fueling the verbal abuse Phoebe was experiencing both online and off.

Annie complained to school officials in early January, but they did nothing. On January 14, Phoebe asked for permission to leave school early because, as she told one of her friends, she had been threatened with being beaten up after school. Faculty denied her request.

When Phoebe came home from school that day, something snapped. The 911 call from Phoebe's family was made at 4:40 PM. According to South Hadley police chief David J. Labrie, "They discovered a teenage girl who appeared to have taken her own life."

As a dozen police cars pulled up to the house in South Hadley, Annie was crying hysterically. At the time, no one outside the school could imagine such a tragic end for a vibrant young woman with a bright future ahead of her.

On January 22, 2010, this obituary appeared in *The Republican* newspaper:

Phoebe Nora Mary Prince
1994–2010 SOUTH HADLEY

> Our beloved daughter Phoebe Nora Mary Prince died tragically on Thursday, January 14, 2010. Phoebe was gifted with exceptional beauty—but that is not important. She was gifted with a sharp and creative brain—but that is not important. She had impressive artistic talent—but that is not important. What her family and friends from both sides of the Atlantic grieve in is the loss of the incandescent enthusiasm of a life blossoming. Phoebe was born in Bedford, England, on Thursday, 24 November, 1994. At the age of two she moved to County Clare, Ireland, where she enjoyed life with an energy only the young possess. At age 14 the family moved to South Hadley, MA, so that Phoebe could experience America and be near family, especially her Uncle John, Auntie Eileen, and cousins Brendan and Molly. Here she touched many lives with her Irish mannerisms and sense of humor. Phoebe will forever live in the hearts of her many friends here in America and Ireland, in particular her dearest friend Cliodhna, from Doolin, County Clare. Phoebe leaves behind her mother Anne Obrien Prince, father Jeremy Prince, sisters Lauren, Tessa and Bridget and brother Simon. Private services and Mass were held January 18 in South Hadley. Additional services will be held in Ireland. A memorial scholarship will be created in Phoebe's name. At this time the family asks that any

> donations be sent to the Phoebe Prince Scholarship Fund at Peoples Bank, 494 Newton Street, South Hadley, MA 01075. "Go gcoinni Dia i mbos a laimhe thu" ("Appointments to God in his hands").

The school posted a notice on its website explaining that a freshman student had taken her life. While no reason for the suicide was given, a number of students were well aware of the tragic circumstances, and someone posted the word "accomplished" on Facebook the night of Phoebe's death. When another student posted that the comment was in poor taste, she was told, "[Y]ou'd better watch your back."

Talk centered around Phoebe for weeks. A student named Sharon Velazquez, 16, was overheard saying she "wasn't the only person that caused Prince's death and that she didn't care that she was dead." Yet another student posted a message about Phoebe on Facebook: "She brought it on herself." Similar posts appeared on other profiles and webpages but were quickly removed.

Gus Sayer, then-superintendent of South Hadley Public Schools, went on record as saying, "Bullying is not tolerated at this school," though he would later admit that bullying played a big part in Phoebe's suicide.

One week after Phoebe's death, then-principal Dan Smith sent a letter to parents explaining that the bullying Phoebe endured had been relationship-related. He claimed that staff took action and "both counseled and provided consequences as the situations required."

"These disagreements centered on relationship-dating issues, a rather common event among high school students," Smith wrote. "Because of the aforementioned disagreements, some students (to be confirmed through investigations) made mean-spirited comments to Phoebe in school and on the way home from school, but also through texting and social networking websites. This insidious, harassing behavior knows no bounds. The key is how each of us deals with that anger—finding ways to resolve or accept differences of opinion instead of engaging in the insidious behavior of demeaning others."

Many parents in the small community of 17,000 found Smith's letter to be too little too late. Town and school meetings took place;

townspeople and parents were angry. Accusing fingers were pointed in every direction, and once the media was involved, Phoebe's suicide soon became fodder for international headlines. Celebrities including Bill Cosby and Khloe Kardashian shared their thoughts publicly.

In an interview on *Larry King Live* on CNN, Cosby said, "I don't know if 'shocked' is the word as … as much as I just did not believe. I don't believe that you can take a job as a teacher, as a superintendent, as a principal and … and not recognize, when you're being told by parents (about bullying)."

"The difference is that today these kids are given so many different outlets to bully," Kardashian wrote on her website. "When I was a child and being teased, we didn't have Twitter, Facebook, or Myspace, so bullying only went on during school hours. Now kids go to school and are tortured, and they come home and still have to deal with it online—there's no escape."

In response to the public outcry, Facebook took action, initiating a 24-hour police hotline, an education and awareness campaign, and a redesigned abuse reporting system, as well as changes to its privacy settings. Many people have urged Facebook to add a panic button for teens to push to report bullies, and the company responded in 2012 by changing the way bullying posts or profiles are reported. Teens can now click on "This post is a problem" and answer a series of simple questions to properly address the situation. There are also links teens can click on if they feel suicidal, which lead to a Facebook suicide hotline and professionals who can help.

In late March 2010, Massachusetts legislators voted a groundbreaking anti-bullying bill into law. The legislation makes bullying illegal at schools, on school buses, and through electronic devices such as mobile phones, email, and internet social networking sites. It outlaws retaliation against people who report bullying to authorities and requires training for teachers and school staff. The law came too late for Phoebe, but it holds promise in protecting other young victims.

In April 2010, school authorities released some essays Phoebe had completed as class assignments; in them, she shared the anguish she'd endured before taking her own life.

In a book report about the book *Cutting*, written by psychotherapist Steven Levenkron, Phoebe wrote, "This book I really connected with as I found there was truth in every word. … It helped me comprehend what people close to me have gone through. Self-mutilation is about trying to transfer the pain from emotional to physical."

In another essay titled "Mind Over Matter," Phoebe wrote, "Where have today's values gone? We live in an impersonal electronic society … Now that we have Twitter and Facebook."

A Facebook group, R.I.P Phoebe Prince, was created in memory of Phoebe. More than 18,000 people have joined the group to date, and other similar forums have been created on Facebook and also on Myspace. The media has increasingly been highlighting the dangers of bullying, including cyberbullying, and states have begun enacting tough new laws. Middle and high schools now regularly offer students and parents advice from experts, much of it geared to recognizing the signs of bullying, letting kids know it's okay to speak out, identifying places they can turn to, and teaching them how to keep it from escalating.

David Hall, PhD, has developed a 99-cent iPhone application called "Bully Shield." "There are right things and wrong things that parents can do to help their children when they are being bullied," says Hall. "Bully Shield is for kids being bullied, family members who care about them, teachers, and school administrators. Bully Shield provides research-based solutions that will reduce the chance your kid is bullied and give you concrete steps to take if your child is being bullied."

Six individuals accused of contributing to Phoebe's death were formally indicted on March 29, 2010. All pled not guilty to the initial charges, and all were expelled from South Hadley High School. The trial concluded May 5, 2011, when five of the six accepted a plea deal. The exception was Renaud, for whom all charges were dropped at the request of Phoebe's parents. The defendants and charges were as follows:

- Mulveyhill and Narey were 17 at the time of the crime and charged as adults. Both were charged with violation of civil rights resulting in bodily injury, criminal harassment, and disturbing a school assembly; Mulveyhill was also charged with statutory rape. Both pled guilty to a misdemeanor charge of criminal harassment and were sentenced to a year of probation and ordered to perform 100 hours of community service; the other charges were dropped. While the harassment charge against Narey was dropped after completion of probation in 2012, the misdemeanor against Mulveyhill will remain on his criminal record.

- Ashley Longe (who was determined to be Phoebe's primary tormentor by the judge), Mullins, and Velazquez were all 16 at the time of the crime and therefore charged as juveniles. All three were charged with criminal harassment, civil rights violations resulting in bodily injury, and disturbing a school assembly; Longe was also charged with assault, and Mullins and Velazquez with stalking. All "admitted to sufficient facts" on misdemeanor charges of harassment, violating civil rights (absent the bodily injury), and disturbing a school assembly; the other charges were dropped. Each received a year of probation and was ordered to perform community service (50 hours for Velazquez; 100 hours for Longe and Mullins). The terms of probation were satisfied, and the charge against each was dismissed without criminal record.
- Renaud, 18, was charged with statutory rape, but the charge was later dropped at the request of Phoebe's family.

Unfortunately, even with all the recent attention, cases such as Phoebe's are far from rare. Carla Carey, of Foxboro, Massachusetts, recently told *People* magazine, "My daughter said things like, 'I can't go on,' and 'Nobody will help me and nobody can help me.'" After reading about what happened to Phoebe, Carey found help for her daughter. "I learned the warning signs," she said. "Phoebe Prince's suicide saved my daughter's life."

***

In another case that received widespread media coverage, 13-year-old Megan Meier of Missouri killed herself in 2006 after a boy she met on Myspace first befriended her and then cruelly taunted her. The "boy" was actually Lori Drew, an adult woman who sought retribution after Megan broke off a friendship with Drew's daughter. Shockingly, Drew knew Megan had issues with depression. In the last message she sent her under the guise she'd created, Drew said, "You are a bad person and everybody hates you ... The world would be a better place without you."

Three weeks before her 14th birthday, Megan wrapped a belt around her neck and hanged herself in her bedroom closet.

On May 15, 2008, Drew was indicted by the Grand Jury of the U.S. District Court on four counts: The first was an allegation of conspiracy, that sometime in September 2006 through October 16, 2006, Drew and her co-conspirators intentionally accessed a computer used in interstate commerce "without authorization," in "excess of authorized use," and used interstate communication to obtain information from the computer in order to inflict emotional distress. The other three counts alleged that on September 20 and 26, and October 16, 2006, Drew accessed Myspace to obtain information regarding Megan, in breach of the Myspace Terms of Service.

On May 16, the state of Missouri passed Senate Bill 818, also known as the Megan Meier Bill, in order to provide "additional protections for Missouri children and adults from being harassed or stalked over the Internet or through other communication devices." It became effective August 28, 2008.

On November 26, 2008, the jury deadlocked on the first count and found Drew guilty of a misdemeanor violation of the Computer Fraud and Abuse Act but not guilty on the other three counts. A judge later dismissed the misdemeanor charge.

Some lawmakers, including Rep. Linda Sanchez (D-Calif.), sought increased protection on April 2, 2009, making the Megan Meier Cyberbullying Prevention Act, H.R. 1966, a federal law. It remains in limbo due to controversy over the broad wording, which includes criminalizing any online communication done "with the intent to coerce, intimidate, harass, or cause substantial emotional distress to a person."

Megan's mother, Tina, launched a website for the Megan Meier Foundation in December 2007. Today, she travels around the country talking about what happened to her daughter, trying to raise awareness of the cyberbullying problem.

***

South Hadley High School now addresses bullying in several places in its Student Handbook, including the following:

- Pages 43–44: Bullying is identified as a "Group C" behavior; minimum consequences include a parent conference, police involvement, and external suspension. Excerpt: "Consequence: Minimum – parent conference and police involvement; risk assessment; after-school education programs as appropriate, external suspension from school. Additional action – Long-term suspension from school, mandated counseling, initiation of expulsion procedures, criminal action, or other administrative actions as required, internal suspension if available, community/school service as applicable if mutually agreed upon."
- Page 56: Bullying is defined as "a negative and often aggressive or manipulative act or series of acts by one or more people against another person or people usually over a period of time. It is abusive and is based on an imbalance of power."

There is also a section called "Types of Bullying," which defines physical, nonphysical, and verbal acts of bullying but does not specifically address cyberbullying or the use of the internet or electronic devices to bully. However, page 57 refers to a Massachusetts law, Chapter 265: An Act Relative to the Crime of Criminal Harassment, Section 43A. Here's an excerpt:

> Whoever willfully and maliciously engages in a knowing pattern of conduct or series of acts over a period of time directed at a specific person, which seriously alarms that

> person and would cause a reasonable person to suffer substantial emotional distress, shall be guilty of the crime of criminal harassment and shall be punished by imprisonment in a house of correction for not more than two and one-half years or by a fine of not more than $1000.00 or by both such fine and imprisonment. Such conduct or acts described in this paragraph shall include, but not be limited to, conduct or acts conducted by mail or by use of a telephonic or telecommunication device including, but not limited to, electronic mail, internet communications, or facsimile communications.

While progress is clearly being made, it's terribly sad that it's taken the deaths of children like Phoebe and Megan to finally get effective anti-bullying legislation on the books.

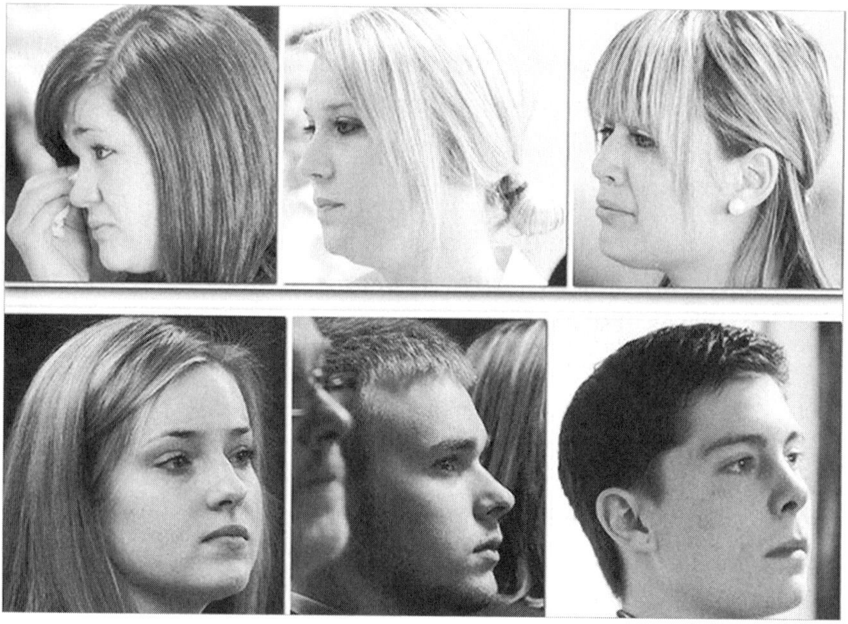

Defendants accused of driving Phoebe Prince to suicide through cyberbullying: [Top row, from left] Ashley Longe, Flannery Mullins, Sharon Velazquez; [Bottom row, from left] Kayla Narey, Sean Mulveyhill, Austin Renaud [©2011 The Republican Company. All rights reserved. Reprinted with permission.]

Phoebe Prince's mother, Anne O'Brien, delivers an impact statement in court [©2011 The Republican Company. All rights reserved. Reprinted with permission.]

Phoebe Prince, whose suicide received international attention [Undated family photo]

Megan Meier, who was tormented by someone she thought was a peer but turned out to be the mother of a former friend [Courtesy of the Megan Meier Foundation, www.meganmeierfoundation]

12

YouTube as Witness

Lisa Kelley parked her car in front of the local drugstore and waited for her friend, Victoria "Tori" Lindsay, to appear. Tori had called just a few minutes earlier, saying she needed a ride home. But when she climbed into the front seat, Tori was battered, bruised, and bloody.

Kelley was shocked. When she asked what had happened, 16-year-old Tori recounted a tale of terror and betrayal. Five of her so-called friends, ranging in age from 14 to 17, had assaulted her while another girl videotaped the beating. These weren't just any girls; these were fellow cheerleaders on her high school squad. To make sure the girls had time to finish the job, two other "friends," Stephen Schumaker and Zachary Ashley, stood guard at the front stoop of the house in case anyone showed up asking what all the commotion was about.

The voices in the background of the video told the story. As the girls took turns pummeling Tori, they screamed at her, blaming her for spreading rumors about them.

"It's not fair, Brittini!" Tori yelled.

"It's perfectly fair! It's one-on-one!" someone replied off-camera.

"You have to fight back. Fight back!" Brittini Hardcastle said as she punched her again. "What, you gonna cry like a little girl?"

"Ooh, yeah, baby. Ooh, yeah!" someone taunted in the background.

Britney Mayes was keeping time. "Seventeen seconds left. Make it good."

For a few weeks before the ordeal, Tori had been staying with her friend Mercades Nichols and her family in Lakeland, Florida. Tori had been struggling with some problems at home and figured the time away from her family would give her a chance to sort things out. By March 30, 2008, Tori was ready to head home. She spent the day at Cocoa Beach with another friend, Christine Dorsett, who dropped her off in the front of Nichols's house.

After the day at the beach, Tori was all smiles when she walked in the front door. Nichols and Hardcastle were waiting for her near the doorway. They were yelling, "Get out! Go home!" It didn't take long for Tori to turn around and run out with the two girls trailing behind her. Then Kayla Hassell suddenly appeared and tagged along behind Nichols and Hardcastle. Luckily, Dorsett was still there; she told the girls to leave Tori alone.

Once everyone had calmed down, Dorsett asked the girls point-blank if there would be any more trouble. She didn't like the thought of leaving Tori behind, but she had to be somewhere and the situation appeared to be under control.

After Dorsett left, Tori went back into the house to gather her belongings and call Kelley for a ride. When she entered her room, April Cooper was waiting with clenched fists. Then Mayes arrived with a camcorder, and Nichols trailed behind her. Hardcastle and Hassell followed Nichols, while Cara Murphy blocked the door. Together, the girls goaded Cooper into hitting Tori. She did just that, again and again.

Tori felt the fists pounding her face. Then Cooper grabbed her head and slammed it into the wall, causing her to black out. When she regained consciousness, she found herself on the living room couch surrounded by the six girls. As she struggled to get up, Hardcastle attacked her. Then, Mayes held her down, and Hassell took over hitting her. Tori finally managed to get loose and run for the door, but Nichols got there first and blocked her escape.

"You want me to leave, I'll go home," Tori cried.

"No, you're not leaving," Hardcastle yelled, knocking her into a corner by the door, next to a glass shelf filled with knickknacks.

"Don't hit the shelves!" Nichols yelled.

One of the boys at the front door told the girls to keep the noise down; the neighbors were getting suspicious and were peering out of their windows.

Tori made another run for the door, but one by one, the girls punched and taunted her, telling her how they planned on posting the video on Myspace and YouTube.

When the beating finally ended about 30 minutes later, the girls forced Tori to pose for group photos with them. When the photo session was over, Nichols threw a bag at Tori that contained her belongings and told her to sit in Nichols's grandmother's car, which was parked in the driveway. Dazed and fearful, Tori limped to the car and climbed into the passenger seat; Mayes and Hardcastle climbed into the backseat as Nichols settled in behind the wheel. In an unprecedented gesture of kindness, one of the girls gave Tori a soda; the other consoled her half-heartedly, saying her injuries weren't all that bad. Nichols told Tori not to breathe a word about this to anyone. Tori snapped back, saying she was going to tell her parents. With that, the girls told her this beating would be nothing compared to the beating she would get if she said anything.

Tori decided to play along and promised to keep her mouth shut. She asked if she could use someone's cell phone to call for a ride home from wherever the girls decided to drop her off. Nichols dropped Tori off at the drugstore, where she waited for Kelley.

When the girls finally made it to Kelley's house, Tori called the police. The following is a partial transcript of the 911 call:

> *Dispatcher*: "Polk County Sheriff's Office, this is Brenda. What is the nature of your emergency?"
> *Tori* (crying): "I just got jumped."
> *Dispatcher*: "You just got what, jumped?"
> *Tori*: "Yes Ma'am."
> *Dispatcher*: "And do you know who did it?"
> *Tori*: "Yes, I do."
> Dispatcher: "What's your name? Okay and where are you?"
> *Tori* [muted]: "I am at my friend's house."

Dispatcher: "Pardon?"

Tori: "I am at my friend's house in Lakeland. Do you need the address?"

Dispatcher: "Yes, ma'am."

Tori: "Okay hold on."

Friend's mother: "Hi I am the Mom. I am not her mom, but the friend's mom."

Dispatcher: "That's okay. Is she hurt?"

Friend's mother: "Yeah I think she—she has a big old knot on the side of her eye."

Dispatcher: "Okay. And who was it that jumped her?"

Friend's mom (to Tori): "They need to know who jumped you."

Tori (in background): "I am going to write all the names down."

Friend's mom: "She is going to write all the names down."

Dispatcher: "So there was more than one?"

Friend's mom: "Yeah. There were six girls. If not more, she said."

Mrs. Kelley gave the dispatcher a list of Tori's injuries: Her mouth was bleeding, her eye was swollen, and one of her teeth was broken.

Kelley took Tori home and she was reunited with her family. When police arrived at Tori's home to interview her and her mother, Talisa, a few days later on April 2, the officer reported, "I witnessed Victoria to have two black eyes, as well as to have bruises on her arms and legs."

He took photos of Tori's injuries and then sat down with her and her mother to take their statements. Tori told him that before she went to Cocoa Beach for the day with Dorsett, she'd argued with Nichols, who was upset that Tori had used her razor and hairbrush without permission. While Tori was at the beach, Nichols sent her several angry text messages. One text accused her of owing Nichols $4 for gas. Oddly, the tone of the messages suddenly softened a few minutes later. Nichols texted Tori, asking when she was coming home. Although Tori was a little suspicious, she was also relieved that

Nichols didn't seem to be holding a grudge. As it turned out, that wasn't the case.

At a news conference in front of Tori's Florida home, Tori's father, Patrick Lindsay, said, "In the emergency room, I didn't even recognize my own daughter. I just walked in and held her. I didn't want her to see me weep."

By the end of that day, six of the teens who had participated in the beating were arrested and placed in holding cells at the sheriff's office.

"I was in my office next to the holding cell and could hear the girls laughing, joking, playing," according to one officer's notes in the report file, "and at one point making the comment, 'Guess we're not going to the beach tomorrow.'"

While an officer was completing Hassell's booking sheet, he remembers her asking, "Am I going to be out of jail in time for cheerleading practice, because I do competitive cheering" and could not miss a single practice.

At one point, the girls said if they were going to get in trouble, then "Steve-O" needed to be arrested, too. The next morning, Schumaker was apprehended and arrested at his parents' home for his part in the ordeal. Ashley was arrested on July 12.

When officers interviewed Nichols's grandmother, Mary Nichols, she told them she didn't know about the fight until later that same night, when Nichols made it sound as if it had been just a little tiff. After talking with Nichols's mother, she found out how vicious the fight was, saw the video, and turned it over to the sheriff's office.

Nichols's mother, Christina Garcia, told the officers that the girls didn't like Tori and were upset because she had reportedly posted nasty comments about them on Myspace.

"She said she was going to kick their you-know-what's," Garcia said, adding that Tori had reportedly called them "slutty," though no such comment was ever found on Myspace or elsewhere.

What Garcia didn't tell officers was that she had taken her daughter's cell phone and some other items out of the house. When officers found out about this, they called her and explained that if she was hiding the cell phone from the police, she was actually withholding evidence, which was a crime. She needed to turn the phone over to the sheriff's office immediately.

Garcia refused to cooperate and even swore at the police. When the officer told her that she could be arrested for tampering with evidence, she promptly hung up on him.

Apparently, Garcia soon had a change of heart. She called the Polk County Sheriff's Office and turned the cell phone in to them later that day.

On April 8, Nichols's home computer was seized as evidence, as well as the other suspects' cell phones. The police also contacted Myspace, and the accounts of all eight suspects, along with Tori's, were frozen so authorities could review them and use any posts as evidence in the case.

The beating changed Tori in many ways: She had a concussion and suffered permanent hearing loss in her left ear, blurred vision in her left eye, and frequent nightmares.

All eight suspects were charged with felony battery and felony false imprisonment. Hardcastle, Mayes, and Nichols were also charged with felony kidnapping for forcing Tori into the car, which carries a maximum penalty of life in prison.

During a press conference in June 2008, Nichols's lawyer James Holz asked, "Why is my client facing life in prison when the victim got two black eyes?"

Nichols's woes escalated in August 2008 when she was arrested on multiple counts of aggravated stalking, aggravated assault, and battery, charges unrelated to Tori's case. Nichols's ex-boyfriend, Jacob Johns, claimed that between October 31, 2007, and March 28, 2008, she allegedly stalked him online and in person, and stabbed him with a pen. She was booked into Polk County Jail and charged with two counts of felony aggravated stalking, two counts of aggravated assault with a deadly weapon, and three counts of misdemeanor battery. She was denied bail.

On January 20, 2009, Mayes pled guilty to one charge of misdemeanor battery in Tori's case. She received a year of probation and was required to complete 50 hours of community service.

On March 6, Nichols pled guilty to battery charges and tampering with a witness in Tori's beating case, and she also pled guilty to the charges of battery, assault, and violation of an injunction in the stalking of her ex-boyfriend. She received 3 years' probation and 100 hours of community service. She was also required to write a letter of apology to Tori and pay $17,000 in restitution to Tori's family. Under the terms of the final verdict, she could never contact Tori or her family, and she could not have an account on any social networking sites, including Facebook, Myspace, and YouTube, during her probation period.

On March 11, Cooper pled guilty to two counts of misdemeanor battery and was sentenced to 2 years' probation in Tori's case. Hassell pled guilty to one count of misdemeanor battery and was sentenced to a year of probation. In addition, both girls had to write a letter of apology to Tori, could never contact Tori or her family, and could not have profiles on social networking sites during their probations. They were also ordered to pay Tori's family $1,752.35, though terms of the case didn't disclose the details of this payment.

On March 20, Hardcastle pled guilty to false imprisonment and battery and was sentenced to 15 days in jail minus time served (10 days), and 3 years' probation. The reason for the stiffer sentence is that on the video she was clearly the one who hit Tori the most. Before she was sentenced, Hardcastle said, "I am very sorry for what I did and nothing will ever excuse it. Me and her didn't get along, but she didn't deserve what she got."

Charges against Murphy, Schumaker, and Ashley were eventually dropped due to lack of sufficient evidence. Tori's parents took her out of high school, and she was homeschooled after the ordeal.

"These websites are creating a space for criminal activity, beating, fights," Tori's father said. "Myspace, YouTube, MTV's *Jackass*—they are enticing our children and desensitizing our children. Now, if they create the best shock video, they are the heroes. They think it is top dollar."

Three minutes of the half-hour video actually ended up on YouTube (you can see it there to this day at www.youtube.com/watch?v=RHmnzzUJVRA), released by the Polk County Sheriff's

Office. While the six girls ultimately got their wish to have the video posted on YouTube, they could never have foreseen it being shown as a cautionary tale for parents and teens.

"Our goal is not only to deal with this issue, but to try to educate parents across the state and across the nation that this is what your children are watching," Polk County sheriff Grady Judd said about releasing the video. "This is what some children are participating in. And we as a society have got to say, 'This has to stop,' because if we desensitize our children to this today, then what's next tomorrow?"

Tori is just one victim whose beating was videotaped for a few minutes of glory in the spotlight.

***

In Thomasville, North Carolina, Daniel Lee Hopkins, 49, thought it would be fun to take part in a video of his 17-year-old son and a 15-year-old boy fighting. All three were arrested on June 10, 2010.

Police had received an anonymous call on June 3 from someone claiming that a video called Dump Fight had been posted on YouTube. It appeared to depict two minors fighting while other people stood around and urged them on.

"We got a tip and went to YouTube and watched it," sheriff David Grice said. "From there we were able to issue a warrant. We've got video of the dad there encouraging [the fight]."

Hopkins was charged with two counts of contributing to the delinquency of a minor and one count of disorderly conduct. His son and the other boy were charged with one count of simple affray and one count of disorderly conduct.

"I've never seen anything like this before," said Grice.

It's not just happening in the U.S., either. In 2010, two teen boys from a high school in Melbourne, Victoria, Australia, were shown in a video being egged on to fight each other. The video was discovered in May 2011 when someone sent the YouTube link to Hampton Park Secondary College principal Sue Glenn. The video had been posted in January 2011.

"I was completely unaware of this incident or video. However, on now seeing it, I am totally appalled," said Glenn. "This is not the behavior we accept at Hampton Park Secondary, which has 1,300 students who are well behaved and great kids. I will be taking this matter extremely seriously and definitely investigating this incident and then taking the appropriate action."

Although the two students fighting in the video no longer attended the school, the onlookers were investigated concerning their involvement. In the video, the witnesses encourage the two boys with shouts of "Go crazy at him" and "Do it, do it" along with a lot of "ooohs" and "whoas," getting louder when one boy's nose starts to bleed.

Victoria's minister for education Martin Dixon noted that having the videos of schoolyard fights and bullying posted made it more difficult to dole out the proper discipline.

"We still have a real issue out there in our schools and we still need to be doing more in terms of educating our children and teachers and parents," said Dixon. "It shows an abject ignorance to what bullying and violence is doing to victims."

By May 2011, the damaging consequences of this incident and others like it triggered the approval of a $14.5 million Australian anti-bullying program that is designed to prevent such behavior from ever starting.

Defendants charged in the videotaped beating of Tori Lindsay: [Top row, from left] April Cooper, Brittini Hardcastle, Kayla Hassell, Britney Mayes; [Bottom row, from left] Cara Murphy, Mercades Nichols, Zachary Ashley, Stephen Schumaker) [Courtesy of Polk County Sheriff's Office]

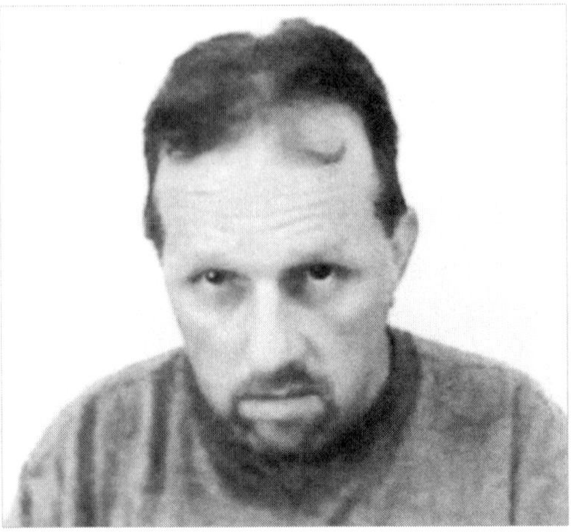

Daniel Lee Hopkins, who videotaped his sons fighting [Courtesy of Davidson County Sheriff's Office]

13

They'll Be Watching You ... Online

When Keri McMullen and her fiancé managed to get tickets to a much-coveted concert in March 2010, she was so excited that she decided to share the good news with her friends.

"I posted that on my Facebook page," Keri said, "who the band was, where we were going. The band started at 8." And so did the robbery. Keri came home to a near-empty house; more than $10,000 worth of items had been stolen. What the burglars didn't know was that Keri's fiancé had recently installed security cameras. He wanted to keep tabs on the house, which was on the market, after someone broke a wineglass during an open house for realtors. No one confessed to breaking the glass, so he installed the cameras.

This technology was definitely lucky for Keri but not so lucky for the burglars. She posted the video on Facebook of the burglars going through the house, rummaging through her purse and drawers, and dumping the laundry out of a basket so they could use it to transport the smaller items. Included in the heist were a plasma TV, a PlayStation, Xbox, laptop, and DVDs.

As fate would have it, one of Keri's 500 Facebook friends actually recognized one of the burglars on the videotape, who turned out to be someone Keri hadn't seen in more than 20 years. Keri had added him to her Facebook friends list just 6 months before.

"I will never ever again put that I'm going anywhere on Facebook," Keri said. "You really don't know who your friends are."

Think you know all of your friends on your friends list and all of your followers? Think again. Criminals are watching what is being posted on walls, feeds, and blogs, and they are just waiting for the perfect opportunity to stop by your place when they know you're not at home.

Just ask Matt Chapman, who tweeted that he was going camping in July 2009 and then posted the news on Facebook. He returned to find that his home had been robbed.

"I never considered the dangers or the ramifications until we were burglarized," he said.

He posted about the experience on his blog:

> Although it is a new trend to communicate "what you are doing" on twitter, or updating your status on facebook, I have a message of caution for everyone who enjoys using social networking sites ... The robber broke into our house through a side window away from our street. Once inside, this jerk stole our Playstation 2 stuff, Game Cube stuff, Amies jewelry, some of my editing software, and worse of all ... my Macbook Pro. My Macbook was loaded with several video projects including everything pertinent to my new business that is still in development called GurillaTV. Luckily I was able to recover everything missing, but it was a real setback. Not to mention the $8,000 of things taken away from us.

***

A webcam came in handy for 12-year-old Hallie Pritchard, who thought her sisters were taking items from her bedroom in November 2011. To catch the thief in the act, she tucked her laptop under the pillows on her bed, positioning the webcam so it would film the entire room.

Hours later when Hallie watched the video, she was shocked. The video showed an unidentified man rifling through her dresser drawers. The video had captured the surprising events when no one had been at home. The man had gained access to her parents' house in

Orinda, California, which had been up for sale. With the video as proof, she showed the footage to her parents, and they immediately contacted police. It didn't take long for the police to apprehend the suspect. Douglas John Calandrella, a former real estate agent, was arrested for stealing jewelry from Hallie's residence. But this wasn't the first time Calandrella had been arrested for such a scheme. The year before, he had taken the keys from several real estate lockboxes, stolen more than 50 items from a number of different houses on the market, and then sold the goods on eBay.

***

In England, Gordon Rayner, a milkman, was convinced that Google Street View helped criminals target his house in a robbery from April 2010. Google Street View included a photo of Gordon's home with the garage door wide open. The image was clear enough that you could see a washing machine and a mountain bike inside.

"When you look at the photograph, my face is blacked out, the windows of my house are blacked out, but because the garage door was left open, you can clearly see everything in there," Gordon said. "I would argue that they should have blacked that out. It is just an invitation for any criminal to take what they like."

The first time the thieves came, they took Gordon's mountain bike. Two days later, the thieves returned but couldn't get into the garage due to a newly installed lock. Gordon has since taken everything out of his garage for safekeeping, except his car.

***

The internet has become a new playground for criminals, who can be some of your so-called friends and fans.

"I'm amazed at how many people get on there and say they're going on vacation," said Lee Struble, head of security at Monroe Community College in Rochester, New York. "Some of these people you haven't seen in 20 or 30 years. But they know where you live or can find out pretty easily; they can do a Google Maps search and can get directions to your house, and you're telling them that you're going to be gone."

The "Digital Criminal Report," which Michael Fraser prepared and released in late 2009, points to social networking and other parts of the internet as vehicles that criminals are using for quick access to easy offerings. Fraser, himself a former thief and now the star of BBC's *Beat the Burglar*, wasn't surprised by any of the findings in the report.

"There is absolutely no doubt in my mind that burglars are using social networks to identify likely targets," Fraser said.

The report surveyed 2,000 social network users and found that nearly two-fifths of the respondents had posted details of holiday/vacation plans, and nearly two-thirds of the 16- to 24-year-old group reportedly posted plenty of details, too. Almost half the respondents reported that they were unconcerned about social networking security. As an experiment, 100 friend requests were issued to random strangers. Nine in 10 Twitter users accepted the stranger as a friend, and more than one in 10 Facebook users did the same, all without asking if they really knew this new person.

"[The criminals] gain confidence by learning more about them, what they are likely to own and when they are likely to be out of the house. I call it 'internet shopping for burglars,'" said Fraser. "It is incredibly easy to use social networking sites to target people, and then scope out more information on their actual home using other internet sites like Google Street View, all from the comfort of the sofa."

Web security firms that have been tracking criminal activity via Twitter and Facebook agree about the correlation between burglaries and social media. "Our research shows that 41 percent of people are divulging personal and private information to complete strangers on Facebook, such as their date of birth, where they worked, where they lived and what they were doing," according to Graham Cluely, senior technology consultant at Sophos, a web security firm. "People are boasting about how they are having a fantastic time on a beach in Mexico on a webpage that has their home address."

***

The FBI has also posted a warning on its website about a new scam that involves momentarily monopolizing phone lines and stealing money from personal bank accounts in the process. These criminals are patient and usually launch the scam weeks or sometimes months before the actual "pounce." There are three primary ways they can gain useful information about a user's financial institution: one, by making phone calls posing as an employee of the institution; two, when the user replies to a phishing email (a typical message advises the user that he must respond to avoid account closure); and three, when the user posts sensitive information in his online profiles.

Equipped with account information and a phone number (business, home, or cell), a savvy thief is able to launch an automatic dialing program that immobilizes the user's phone line, making it appear to be constantly busy. The user suddenly gets a series of unexplained phone calls, or sometimes dead air, or a seemingly random recorded message.

While the target is busy answering these random phone calls, the scammer will either contact the user's financial institution pretending to be the user or access the user's bank account online in order to transfer the money elsewhere. A thief will sometimes log in to an account, change the phone number to the one they're using (most likely for a throwaway cell phone), and then wait for the financial institution to call them to verify the transfer.

In 2009, a Florida periodontist lost nearly $400,000 from his retirement account through such a scam. Robert Thousand Jr. of St. Augustine began receiving hundreds of phone calls from a sex hotline every day for almost a month on his office, home, and cell phone lines in a ploy called a targeted denial of service (TDOS).

"If you are gay, press 1. If you are a lesbian, press 2," a sultry voice said, continuing with other options to choose from for 30 seconds.

"The calls came in so fast that call rollover couldn't handle it," Robert said. "Nobody could get through. The hospital couldn't call me. [Patients] couldn't get through. AT&T's solution was 'just change your number.' Not exactly easy to do for an office."

The doctor traced the events to a business trip he took to the Bahamas just weeks before the phone calls began. He believes someone put a Trojan horse (a destructive program that masquerades as a benign application) on his laptop to obtain private information about his finances and his accounts.

While Robert was answering the calls, withdrawals were being made from his TD Ameritrade account that ranged from $18,000 to $100,000 for a total of $399,000. When he found out, he put a freeze on all of his accounts.

"They knew all my phone numbers, all my credit card numbers," Robert said. "I've been saving for 30 years of working and they wipe me out in a matter of weeks."

Authorities were able to trace the withdrawals to New York City, but the doctor was told that he would probably never see his money again. Robert also discovered that he might have to pay taxes on the money because of the early withdrawal penalty from his retirement account. But he was lucky: In May 2010, all of his money was miraculously returned.

"Following that first incident in November 2009 [Robert's scam], we've seen an increase in this activity targeting our customers across the country," said Adam Panagia, associate director of global fraud management for AT&T. "We urge anyone who suspects they may be the target of a TDOS attack to immediately contact their telephone provider after notifying their financial institutions."

The FBI joined forces with the Communications Fraud Control Association in June 2010 "to analyze the patterns and trends of telephone denial-of-service attacks, educate the public, and identify the perpetrators and bring them to justice."

Law enforcement is using the same tech tools the scammers are using to apprehend these internet-savvy criminals. If the FBI has an unsolved crime where photos or surveillance camera footage is available, many police departments are posting them on Twitter, Facebook, and Myspace along with the question, "Can you ID this armed robbery suspect?" The Boynton (FL) Police Department tried this tactic in June 2009, using social networking to find criminals.

"It's an easy way to reach people very quickly," said Seamus Condron, community manager of Mediabistro.com, an online media and training website. "This is a really large set of eyes and ears that police can call into action."

The police in Boca Raton, Florida, credit social networking with providing an anonymous tip that led to the arrest of 20-year-old Darrien Downey for grand theft. The tipster recognized a photo posted on the police department's Facebook and Myspace pages of a man in a black-and-white-checked flannel shirt stealing a $600 TV from a local mall in February 2009. The tipster's information led police to Downey's Myspace page, where he was wearing the same shirt in many of the photos.

If it hadn't been for Myspace and Facebook, "that kid would probably be out there watching (the stolen) TV right now," said Boca Raton police spokesman Mark Economou.

In June 2010, after the Los Angeles Lakers became NBA champs, police were dealing with citywide property damage from overzealous fans. The police force posted surveillance video from local businesses and TV coverage on Twitter, YouTube, and Facebook. By the end of the first day, the YouTube video had been viewed nearly 250,000 times, and as a result, dozens of people were recognized, identified, and arrested on vandalism charges.

"In the age of phone cameras and digital video devices, it has in essence deputized the public in fighting crime," Lt. Paul Vernon told the *Contra Costa Times*. "It has added to the maxim that police are the public and the public are the police."

Other law enforcement agencies also keep track of Twitter feeds as well as Myspace and Facebook posts from gang members.

"You find out about people you never would have known about before," said Dean Johnston of the California Bureau of Narcotics Enforcement, which helps police investigate gangs. "You build this little tree of people."

In February 2010, a gang member was released from prison and other gang members believed he had cut a deal with police. Posts and tweets appeared warning that there was a snitch among them. Authorities watched these messages and gathered enough incriminating evidence to arrest three gang members on drug charges. Many gang members and criminals enjoy bragging online about their crimes, making threats, and sharing information about rival gangs.

"We are seeing a lot more of it," Johnston said. "They will even go out and brag about doing shootings. Once you get into a Facebook group, it's relatively easy. You have a rolling commentary."

Keri McMullen and her now husband, who shared their vacation plans on Facebook, resulting in the robbery of their home [Courtesy of Keri McMullen Pendleton]

Surveillance footage of the burglary of Keri's home [Courtesy of Keri McMullen Pendleton]

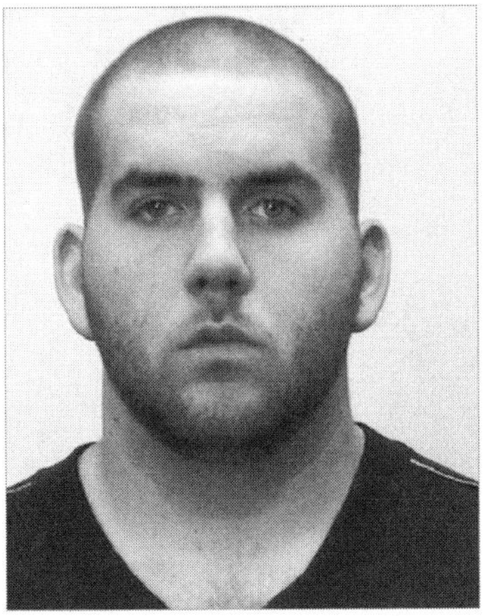

Darrien Downey, a thief captured thanks to social media [Courtesy of Boca Raton Police Department]

Matt Chapman, also a robbery victim after revealing on Facebook that he would be out of town [Courtesy of Matt Chapman]

14

The Killer Inside

Mark Drybrough of Coventry, England, had a long history of depression. In July 2005, the 32-year-old was so despondent that he began looking for information online about how to hang himself. That's when Mark encountered 48-year-old William Melchert-Dinkel, a former nurse who was posing as any one of several alter egos with the names "Li Dao," "Cami," or "Falcon Girl."

"If a person is less than 6 feet tall, you can easily hang from a door using the knob on one side to tie the rope to, sling it over the top of the door, attach the noose or loop to yourself and then step off and hang successfully," Melchert-Dinkel wrote as Li Dao. "A sturdy knot is very much all one needs."

Melchert-Dinkel trolled websites and chat rooms on Google and Yahoo! pretending to be a female nurse. But instead of offering compassion and support, this Minnesota man developed a relationship with his victims and then offered them step-by-step instructions on the best way to commit suicide. Sometimes he made a pact with the victim that he would commit suicide at the same time.

When Melchert-Dinkel found Mark online, they exchanged email until they'd established a seemingly trusting relationship. Melchert-Dinkel, masquerading as Li Dao, offered his usual rounds of compassion and concern, followed by a push to end it all. Although Melchert-Dinkel tried to convince Mark to hang himself in front of a webcam so that he could watch the suicide, Mark refused.

In Mark's final email to Li Dao, he wrote that he was scared and "holding on to the hope that things might change." Four days later on July 27, 2005, Mark's sister found his body hanging in the doorway of his apartment.

Melchert-Dinkel's second victim was 18-year-old Nadia Kajouji of Brampton, Ontario, Canada. She encountered Melchert-Dinkel, assuming the role of Cami, in March 2008. Nadia confided to Cami that she was planning on committing suicide by jumping into a river, adding that "if drowning doesn't get me, hopefully hypothermia will." Cami reached out to Nadia with a proposition: If Nadia couldn't commit suicide by herself, they could make a suicide pact to kill themselves at the same time and be linked together in their final minutes via a webcam. Cami offered her support and encouragement.

On March 9, 2008, Nadia was reported missing by campus security at Carleton University where she was a student. It took Canadian authorities 3 days before they started a search for her whereabouts. Her body was discovered 6 weeks later in the Rideau River; she was wearing ice skates, which most likely weighed her down, making it more difficult to find her.

Melchert-Dinkel didn't get away with his actions for long. Other members of the chat rooms and websites he frequented grew increasingly suspicious about the online communication between Melchert-Dinkel's aliases and the suicides of Mark and Nadia. An unnamed woman from the U.K. contacted authorities at the Internet Crimes Against Children Task Force in St. Paul, Minnesota, because she suspected someone who frequented the same chat rooms as she did was encouraging people to commit suicide.

After receiving this tip, a 2-year investigation ensued as police reviewed the extent of Melchert-Dinkel's chat room conversations. It was only a matter of time before they discovered his connections to Mark and Nadia. When police contacted the victims' family members, they were more than willing to cooperate and turn over what information they had, including computers and printouts of messages between Melchert-Dinkel and his victims.

By April 2010, the St. Paul police arrested Melchert-Dinkel and charged him with two felony counts of aiding suicide in the deaths of

Mark and Nadia. Melchert-Dinkel admitted in court that he participated in online chat room conversations about suicide with as many as 20 people and had entered into fake suicide pacts with at least 10 of them. Five of those who made a suicide pact with him eventually killed themselves, but the police could link him with definitive evidence to just two: Mark and Nadia.

Melchert-Dinkel credited the decision to act on his dark urges as the "thrill of the chase." He admitted that what he did was morally wrong, but he still believed that conversations about suicide such as those he had with the victims were protected under his right to free speech and therefore not illegal. He told police he had an obsession with suicide and death that triggered his behavior. Rice County (MN) district court judge Thomas Neuville decided otherwise.

"The court does find that what you did was stalking, or soliciting people to die," Neuville said. "I think that what you did was calculated, intentional. It was fraudulent. When you use speech in this manner, it's not protected. It's criminal."

On May 4, 2011, Melchert-Dinkel was sentenced to 320 days in jail (with work release, which lets him work during the day but return to prison each night). He was ordered to spend an additional 40 days in jail for 2-day stints during the following decade on the anniversaries of both his victims' deaths, 160 hours of community service (8 hours during the month of each of his victims' deaths over the next 10 years), and a 15-year probation. As part of his sentence, he is prohibited from having internet access (except for work) and can never be employed in the healthcare profession or work with vulnerable adults. He was also ordered to pay $18,000 in fines and about $30,000 in restitution costs to Nadia's family. Mark's family did not seek restitution.

Nadia's brother, who attended the hearing for the sentencing portion of the trial, told CTV Toronto, "A guilty verdict isn't justice. Punishment is justice, and a year in a jail with work release doesn't really seem like justice."

However, Mark's mother, Elaine Drybrough, was satisfied with the sentence. "When I look at it all together, I think it's quite good really. For someone who hasn't been in prison before, I should think a year in prison will make an impression," she stated. "Somebody said to me, 'you must hate him,' but I don't know really—it's difficult. I think he has learnt his lesson. It gives a message if there's other people doing that as well, that they don't necessarily get away with it."

***

In September 2010, the suicide of a student who had recently started classes at Rutgers University in New Jersey made national headlines. Eighteen-year-old Tyler Clementi was proud to be one of the incoming students at Rutgers that semester. He lived on campus with his roommate Dharun Ravi, and life was good, or at least he thought it was. Ravi was pleasant and helpful to Tyler when they were together, but Ravi displayed quite different behavior online and behind Tyler's back.

On September 19, 2010, Ravi tweeted about Tyler's after-hours activities: "Roommate asked for the room till midnight. I went into Molly's room and turned on my webcam. I saw him making out with a dude. Yay."

Molly was Molly Wei, one of Ravi's friends. While Ravi remotely accessed his laptop webcam in the room he shared with Tyler, Ravi and Wei watched Tyler's intimate moments with another male student.

According to a report first published on the Gawker gossip website, a post made on September 21 in a gay-themed chat room appeared to be from Tyler going by the screen name "cit2mo." He described how he had found a webcam that had captured his encounters with another male student and then read the tweet on his roommate's Twitter feed. He wondered about what he should do and the best way to handle the situation.

The person posting the message, who was later assumed to be Tyler, wrote: "don't wanna report him and then end up with nothing happening except him getting pissed at me."

Two days later, Ravi was back to his old tricks. He tweeted, "Anyone with iChat, I dare you to video chat me between the hours of 9:30 and 12. Yes it's happening again."

Although it appears that no one actually watched the second webcast, Tyler posted in a chat room that he had unplugged Ravi's computer and searched for any possible hidden microphones, thinking he was safe. He also asked his resident advisor to assign him to another roommate, but Tyler grew more upset just knowing that people had seen the first webcast and perhaps the second one, as well.

On September 22, Tyler posted on his Facebook wall via his cell phone, "Jumping off the gw bridge sorry." Tyler jumped to his death from the George Washington Bridge the same day that Ravi's Twitter account mysteriously disappeared.

After authorities interviewed students in Tyler's dormitory, the crime was deemed more than just a suicide. By the end of September, Ravi and Wei, both 18, had been charged with two counts of invasion of privacy for using "the camera to view and transmit a live image" of Tyler, carrying a maximum sentence of 5 years. Ravi was also charged with two additional counts of invasion of privacy for the second webcam broadcast.

Tyler's family issued a statement to the media that read in part, "Tyler was a fine young man, and a distinguished musician. The family is heartbroken beyond words."

On April 20, a New Jersey grand jury indicted Ravi on hate crime charges for streaming the webcast of Tyler's romantic encounter with another man. That meant he could face 5 to 10 years in prison if convicted, which is a harsher sentence than if he had been convicted of the earlier charges. In addition, Ravi was charged with a cover-up (by deleting his Twitter account to mislead investigators) and trying to convince witnesses not to testify.

"The grand jury charged that the invasion of privacy and attempt to invade the privacy of T.C. [Tyler Clementi] and M.B. [Clementi's romantic interest] were intended to intimidate them because of their sexual orientation," prosecutors said in a statement.

Although not indicted, Wei was charged with invasion of privacy. At a hearing on May 6, she pled not guilty to two counts of invasion of privacy. She was accepted into a pretrial intervention program, which led to a dismissal of all charges against her, wiping her criminal record clean. She also completed 300 hours of community service and received counseling for cyberbullying, as well as testified against Ravi on May 23, 2011.

After the hearing, Rubin Sinins, Wei's lawyer, said, "Molly Wei is not a bully. She has cooperated from the beginning and will continue to cooperate with the investigation and the prosecutor's office."

On March 17, 2012, Ravi was found guilty on all counts, and a few days later, he was sentenced to 30 days in jail, of which he served 20. He was released from jail on June 19, 2012. Ravi was also sentenced to 3 years probation and 300 hours of community service, and he must attend counseling for cyberbullying and acceptance of alternative lifestyles.

Tyler's suicide was only one of many reported during September of 2010. He joined at least eight other young men who committed suicide after being taunted online and offline for allegedly being gay:

Billy Lucas (15) September 9, Indiana
Cody J. Barker (17) September 13, Wisconsin
Seth Walsh (13) September 19, California
Asher Brown (13) September 23, Texas
Harrison Chase Brown (15) September 25, Colorado
Raymond Chase (19) September 29, Rhode Island
Felix Sacco (17) September 29, Massachusetts
Caleb Nolt (14) September 30, Indiana

On October 1, 2010, Arne Duncan, secretary of education for the U.S. Department of Education, addressed the pervading problem in a press release, acknowledging the deaths of two of the victims, Tyler and Raymond, who hanged himself in his dorm at Johnson & Wales University in Providence, Rhode Island.

"This week, we sadly lost two young men who took their own lives for one unacceptable reason: They were being bullied and harassed because they were openly gay or believed to be gay," Duncan said. "These unnecessary tragedies come on the heels of at least three other young people taking their own lives because the trauma of being bullied and harassed for their actual or perceived sexual orientation was too much to bear.

"This is a moment where every one of us—parents, teachers, students, elected officials, and all people of conscience—needs to stand up and speak out against intolerance in all its forms. Whether it's students harassing other students because of ethnicity, disability or religion; or an adult public official harassing the President of the University of Michigan student body because he is gay, it is time we as a country said enough. No more. This must stop."

Nadia Kajouji, who took her life after making a suicide pact with someone she met online—in reality, William Melchert-Dinkel [Courtesy of Alex Schadenberg]

Melchert-Dinkel, eventually convicted in connection to Nadia's case as well as the suicide of Mark Drybrough [Courtesy of St. Paul Police Department]

15

When Revenge and Hatred Are Fueled Online

In the early morning of December 11, 2010, Mark Madoff emailed his wife, Stephanie Madoff, who was vacationing in sunny Florida with their 4-year-old daughter. He was at their apartment in New York City with their 2-year-old son and their dog, dealing with the Northeast's seasonal chill.

At first, their email exchanges covered the usual topics about the kids and the dog, but then Stephanie noticed a decidedly different tone in Mark's responses. He wrote that she "would be better off without 'this' hanging over them all, forever." A few minutes later, he wrote, "You'll have a better life if I'm not around … I love you." The last email he sent asked her to send someone to check on their son and their dog.

Stephanie called her father, who rushed to Mark and Stephanie's Soho apartment at 7:27 AM. When he entered the home, he found his 46-year-old son-in-law hanging from a steel pole supporting a lighting rack mounted on the living room ceiling. Mark had used his dog's leash as a noose.

Mark's father was Bernie Madoff, who pled guilty to 11 federal felonies for defrauding a seemingly endless list of unsuspecting investors. Bernie admitted that his longtime business was actually a giant Ponzi scheme—a fraudulent investment operation that pays returns to investors not from any actual profit earned by the organization but from their own investments and those of subsequent investors. As most Americans are aware, Bernie's scheme eventually imploded, but before everything came crashing down it's unlikely he ever imagined the toll his financial improprieties would take on his family. He certainly could not have foreseen his son's tragic suicide.

Bernie thought his scam was so solid that no one would find out how much money he stole from his clients. But in December 2008, he was arrested on fraud charges, and by the following March he had admitted to having bilked his clients out of $50 billion. On June 29, Bernie received the maximum sentence for his crimes: 150 years in federal prison. The earliest he can be released is November 14, 2139.

This sentence wasn't quite stiff enough for some of his clients. Irving Picard, for instance, who was the trustee in charge of locating assets for Bernie's victims, filed a suit that included Bernie's sons, Mark and Andrew Madoff, who had both worked for their father. Most observers of the case assumed at the time that the sons had also taken tens of millions of dollars to support their lavish lifestyles. Neither was criminally charged, but both were under investigation, as was their uncle, Peter Madoff. Picard filed another suit that included Mark's four children, including two from a previous relationship.

As Mark scoured the internet for information about the legal case, he became distraught by the vitriol that was being directed toward him online, both anonymously and with attribution.

"Mark was an innocent victim of his father's monstrous crime who succumbed to 2 years of unrelenting pressure from false accusations and innuendo," said Mark's attorney, Martin Flumenbaum, after learning of his client's death. "We are all deeply saddened by this shocking turn of events."

An unnamed law enforcement source later said about Mark, "The son knew he was in the cross hairs. At first he thought he would somehow skate, but once [the trustee recovering assets for investors] detailed the family theft, he knew his time was limited."

Although it will never be known to what extent Mark knew about his father's criminal activity, he knew he would eventually have to go to court to testify. Friends speculated that this impending court ordeal was most likely what put him over the edge.

***

In another case, an Arizona teen's hatred of his father also took a deadly turn. Fifteen-year-old Hughstan Schlicker took family matters into his own hands on February 6, 2008. When the call came in to the 911 dispatcher that day, the voice on the other end was anguished.

"I hate my dad, I couldn't take it anymore!" wailed Schlicker, who was calling from his home in Mesa. He then told the dispatcher that he had just shot his father with a 12-gauge shotgun. His father was dead, lying in a pool of blood in the kitchen.

When police arrived on the scene, Schlicker said he had been mad at his father for taking away his internet privileges. His father had seen Schlicker's suicide threats posted on Myspace, a site the young teen frequented. After he punished the boy by refusing to let him online, Schlicker said he couldn't deal with the loss of access to his Myspace account.

"It felt like I was stabbed with a knife and it went straight through and … no matter how hard I pulled, I couldn't pull out the knife," Schlicker said during a police interview.

Schlicker told police that earlier in the day he had pretended to be his father and called out sick to school. He wandered around the house for a while, went to the garage, and found the shotgun. He took the shotgun to his bedroom and had planned on killing himself in front of his father, but then he changed his mind. Instead, he decided to kill his father first, then himself.

Schlicker formulated his game plan in the morning: If his father came home after 4:00 PM, he wouldn't do it. He was going to let fate determine his decision. So he simply sat on the staircase in the house and waited.

Schlicker said he heard the door open about 2:00 PM; his father had come home early. When his father went into the kitchen, Schlicker snuck up behind him and shot his father in the back of the head. Then, instead of killing himself, Schlicker said he called a friend and told her what he had done. She convinced him to call 911.

His mother opened the door to a grisly scene just before the police arrived. In a transcript from police interviews, Schlicker's mother unconditionally supported her son. "I know, I know it happened," she said. "We have to get past this. It's not going to change anything between you and me. You're still my son and I love you no matter what, OK? I'll be there whenever you need me."

Schlicker expressed remorse in the police interview. "I wish I didn't do this," he said. "I miss Dad."

Although he was just 15 at the time of the murder, Schlicker was tried as an adult and charged with first degree murder. He pled guilty to a charge of second degree murder on May 27, 2009, and was sentenced to 20 years in prison on July 10. After his sentencing, Schlicker said, "I'd like to say I'm sorry and I'm scared. I wish my father was still alive and I feel terrible for all this to happen. He didn't deserve this."

***

For some people, the internet offers a way to use and abuse others. A case in point is an Australian man who became known as the "Facebook Killer."

Ramazan Acar posted a status update on his Facebook page on November 18, 2010: "bout to kill ma kid."

The 24-year-old Acar, at home in Melbourne, Australia, violated a court order and appeared at the front door of his estranged girlfriend's house. Acar wanted to take Yazmina (Mimi), his 2-year-old daughter, for a chocolate treat at the local ice cream shop. Her mom, Rachelle D'Argent, couldn't refuse the request.

"If you saw her face when she saw her dad that afternoon, she had stars in her eyes when she ran up to him," D'Argent said. "That's why I let her go with him. I did it for Mimi."

D'Argent grew uneasy when they didn't return 10 minutes later, as promised. When she called Acar on his cell phone, he said he was taking Mimi to McDonald's for another treat and promised to bring her home soon. Instead, he called D'Argent back a few minutes later and taunted her, saying, "How does it feel to not have your child when I did not have mine for three months?" He added, "I loved you, Rachelle, and look what you've made me do."

Acar told D'Argent that he was going to stab Mimi, but she said she didn't believe him, thinking he was just trying to scare her. He was doing a good job of it.

At 7:23 PM, Acar posted another status update on Facebook that he was going to kill his little daughter. Eleven minutes later, he updated his Facebook page again, posting "Pay bk u slut." After Acar's last message, D'Argent finally called the police.

When Acar called D'Argent again at 8:47 PM, he told her that he had done the unthinkable: "She's just lying there next to me in her leggings and her top covered in blood. I killed her to get back at you. Even if I go behind bars I know that you are suffering." He texted D'Argent a few minutes later: "It's ova, I did it."

At 11:20 PM, Acar updated his Facebook page again. "I lv u mimi." Police arrived 10 minutes later to apprehend Acar. Police didn't find Mimi until hours later; her body had been dumped in a grassy area next to a fence near the Greenvale Reservoir. She had been stabbed to death. The coroner's office later reported that the child had suffered a long and slow death. Acar had missed vital organs when he stabbed her, leaving her to die slowly.

D'Argent never explained why she neglected to call police after Acar's first threatening Facebook postings, phone calls, and texts appeared. On May 4, 2011, Acar pled guilty to murder and was sentenced to life in prison on May 18.

Melbourne Magistrates Court justice Elizabeth Curtain stated that life in prison was the only appropriate sentence for Acar, who pled guilty to his crime.

"More than that, the victim was your infant daughter, and she was killed by the one man in the world whose duty it was to love, nurture, and protect her," Curtain said. "As such, your conduct was a fundamental breach of the trust that reposes between parent and child, a fundamental breach of a parent's most fundamental obligation. Further, you committed this murder for the worst possible motives—revenge and spite. You killed your daughter to get back at her mother. You used your daughter, an innocent victim, as the instrument of your overarching desire to inflict pain on your former partner."

***

For some criminals, cyberspace offers a prime opportunity to carry out the ultimate revenge for comments posted online.

In early September 2011, motorists in the northern Mexican town of Nuevo Laredo encountered a horrific site. Two mutilated bodies, a man and a woman, were hanging from a pedestrian footbridge.

The killers left their calling cards on the victims explaining their deeds. A sign attached to the man's leg read [translated into English], "This happened for snitching on Frontera Al Rojo Vivo," referring to an internet forum created to inform about cartel activity.

The sign attached to the woman's body read, "This will happen to all the internet snitches (Frontera al Rojo Vivo, Blog Del Narco, or Denuncia Ciudadano) Be warned, we've got our eye on you."

Both were signed with a "Z," which many believe to be the Los Zetas gang, which allegedly controls Nuevo Laredo.

Both victims were in their 20s. The women's bowels were draped down her body, her breasts exposed, and her hands and feet tied to the bridge; the male victim was hanging from the bridge by his hands. He had a gash so deep that his right shoulder was almost completely severed. Mexican authorities later said that both of the victims had been savagely tortured.

Since 2006, more than 40,000 people have been killed in the wake of the ongoing drug wars in Mexico. Authorities initially thought that using social networking sites as tools for people to report activity was a good idea, at least until these two victims were murdered.

Mexican bloggers were defiant in their posts and tweets in response to the murders, seemingly taunting whoever committed the brutal murders.

It didn't take long for more retaliation to take place. On September 25, 2011, a female blogger was found decapitated in Nuevo Laredo on the side of a main road in town. Maria Elizabeth Macias (aka Marisol Marcias Castaneda), an advertising supervisor at Nuevo Laredo's newspaper, *Primera Hora*, had been posting negative comments about the drug cartels on a local social networking website called Nuevo Laredo Live. The site offers tips for the Mexican army, navy, and police. In exchange for her postings, her decapitated head was placed upon a pile of stones near her body.

A sign had been left near her body in much the same way as with the two other victims: "Nuevo Laredo en Vivo and social networking sites, I'm The Laredo Girl, and I'm here because of my reports, and yours," according to the message found on Castaneda. "For those who don't want to believe, this happened to me because of my actions, for believing in the army and the navy. Thank you for your attention, respectfully, Laredo Girl ... ZZZZ."

Her friends and family claim that she used an anonymous screen name to post her comments. So authorities believe it was someone she knew who revealed her real name to the killers who tracked her down and made her pay the ultimate price for posting her words online.

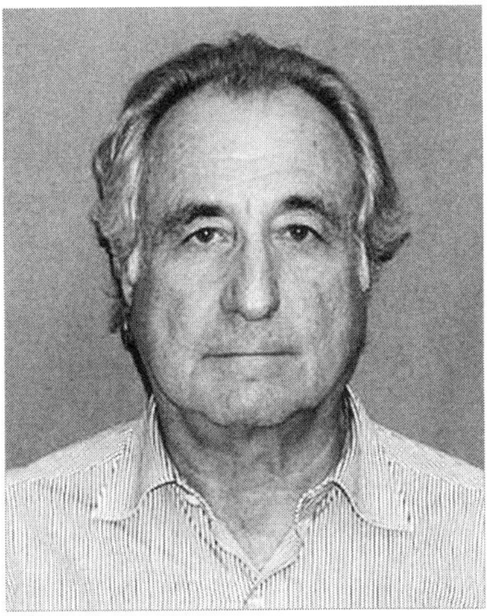

Bernie Madoff, whose son Mark committed suicide after being humiliated online in connection with his father's crimes [Courtesy of U.S. Department of Justice]

Hughstan Schlicker, convicted of murdering his father for taking away his internet privileges [Courtesy of Mesa Police Department]

16

Craigslist Killers

When the deputy sheriff at Boston's Nashua Street Jail entered Philip Markoff's cell on August 14, 2009, he noticed that Markoff was unusually still under the blanket that covered him from head to toe. It was unusual too because it was August. Even Markoff's chest wasn't moving; he didn't seem to be breathing.

The deputy sheriff pulled back the blanket to expose a disturbing scene underneath. The 23-year-old Markoff had tied a plastic bag over his head and wrapped plastic wrap around his arms where he had cut himself. Before he died he'd scrawled his ex-fiancée's name, "Megan," in blood on the cell wall above the door. The two were supposed to have been married that day; instead, it was his last.

Just months earlier Markoff had been leading what by all accounts was a charmed life. A graduate of the State University of New York–Albany as a premed student in 2007, the blond, blue-eyed youth with the engaging smile was in his second year at the Boston University School of Medicine. A member of the Young Republicans, Markoff was engaged to the equally blonde, blue-eyed, and attractive Megan McAllister, whom he'd met as a fellow volunteer at the Albany Medical Center Emergency Room. At the time, Megan was looking forward to starting medical school in 2009.

Markoff seemed to be a "good student and just a really nice kid. Smart, wanting to succeed, nothing strange, nothing out of the ordinary," according to his teachers. He kept his darkest secret buried: He was a killer.

Trisha Leffler discovered Markoff's secret firsthand. On April 10, 2009, as the first signs of spring were sprouting up in the Boston area, the 29-year-old checked in to her room at the Westin Copley Place Hotel in Back Bay and logged on to her laptop. In Las Vegas, police were getting tougher on escort girls, so she decided to leave Vegas and try her luck in Boston. Her first step was to place an ad in the erotic services section on craigslist under "Sweet Blonde."

Working alone was always risky, but Trisha knew the payoff was worth it. She could make thousands of dollars in a week as long as she was careful. She could pick and choose her clients, and it was safer than working the streets.

It didn't take long for her cell phone to ring. She chatted with the caller and felt comfortable enough to give him her room number. At the appointed time, she opened her hotel door to her first client of the day and breathed a sigh of relief.

"He looked nice, he looked young," she said. "Good looking, obviously."

With a flash of his engaging smile, he shut the door and turned to face Trisha. That's when she saw the gun in his hand.

"I backed up a little bit," she said. "He just said, 'If you do everything you're asked, no harm's gonna come to you.' He said, 'Lay down, put your hands behind your back.' When he started to walk towards me, he put the gun back in his pocket."

She thought for a moment that he might just be role-playing and wasn't surprised when he pulled out a pair of black leather gloves and plastic zip ties from his pants pocket. He put the gloves on slowly.

He knelt down in front of her and shoved his knee between her legs. Then he pinned her down and demanded money. She realized he was serious, and she was scared.

Trisha told him that she had about $8,000 in cash, which he let her get and give to him. She also offered up her credit and debit cards. He shoved the bills into his pocket, along with the cards. He grabbed her cell phone, took off his gloves, and removed his phone number from her call list. He saw a pair of her panties on the floor, picked them up, and tucked them into his pocket.

After he walked around the room for a few minutes, he headed to the bathroom and ordered her to come in. He tied her wrists to the doorknob, cut the telephone lines, and then put duct tape over her mouth. She realized at that point that he hadn't put his gloves back on, so his fingerprints were on everything he had touched. Thankfully, he then left.

Trish broke free from the zip ties, but she was afraid to yell for help. She thought he might be waiting outside for her to make a move. When she carefully peered out of the peephole, she couldn't see anyone, so she waited a minute or so, then slowly opened the door. The hallway was empty. She grabbed her room key, closed her door, ran to the next room, and pounded on the door.

When the man in the next room opened the door, Trisha pushed her way into the room. "Can I call security?" she asked. "I've just been robbed at gunpoint."

At first, Trisha was worried that the Boston police wouldn't believe her because she was an escort, but she was wrong. When they arrived at the hotel, the police listened to her story and told her they wanted to apprehend this guy. She went to the station to look at photos and pointed to a surveillance photo from the hotel. It was the man who had robbed her.

Four days later on April 14, Boston police rushed to the Copley Marriott in Boston. A hotel guest on the 20th floor had heard gunshots, run into the hallway, and found a woman staggering out of a room before collapsing on the floor. The guest called hotel security, who alerted local police. When the police arrived, Julissa Brisman's body was lying in the doorway of the room. The 25-year-old had been shot and on her wrist was a zip tie. She was rushed to Boston Medical Center, where she later died from multiple gunshots to her torso. Officers at the scene recalled that these were the same type of zip ties used in Trisha's case. They started looking for a connection between the cases and soon found it. Julissa had also placed an ad on craigslist, for massage services.

Surveillance video from the Copley hotel showed a young man walking calmly and looking at his cell phone. Trisha quickly recognized him as the same man who had robbed her. But now he had murdered a woman. The connection was enough for the media to dub him the "Craigslist Killer."

Two days later, a stripper working under the name of "Amber" placed an ad on craigslist offering private lap dances for $200 in her hotel room at the Holiday Inn in Warwick, Rhode Island. One of the men who responded to the ad knocked on her door. When she checked him out through the peephole, he was young and handsome. She didn't think twice about opening the door and inviting him in.

But when he closed the door, he turned and pointed a gun at her. He looked nervous, and his hand was shaking along with the gun.

"I'm broke," he said. "I don't want to kill you. I just need cards or money."

When she told him that she would give him whatever he wanted, he took zip ties out of his pocket, tied her wrists, and then made her sit on the ground while he ransacked the room.

Her cell phone began to ring again and again. He wanted to know who it was. She didn't reply. Suddenly, the ringing stopped. Amber knew it was her husband, who was also her business manager. He always called when she was with a client to make sure everything was okay. When she didn't answer her cell phone, he knew something was wrong.

Amber's husband ran to his wife's room from the hotel lobby, and as he approached, the door opened. A young man came out with a gun pointed at him. Neither man said a word. Amber's husband ran in one direction, the robber in the other, and Amber slammed the door shut with her elbow. She called hotel security; she knew she had been attacked by the Craigslist Killer.

Amber identified the man in the hotel surveillance video as the same young man in the lobby and stairwell of the Boston hotels.

The police from Boston and Warwick wanted to find the Craigslist Killer before he struck again. Although the photos clearly showed the killer's face, the police couldn't identify him yet.

The big break came when one of Julissa's friends found an email exchange she had with her 10 PM appointment, the man who turned out to be her killer. When Boston police examined the email files and opened the headers of the email to identify the IP address, they were able to trace the computer to an apartment in Quincy, Massachusetts, a suburb of Boston. The apartment belonged to Markoff.

Police weren't sure whether Markoff was actually the Craigslist Killer. After all, he was a second-year medical student. To be certain, they set up a stakeout in front of Markoff's apartment building.

On April 19, Markoff left the apartment building with Megan, and headed for a car parked on the street. He perfectly matched the description of the man in the surveillance videos.

An officer noticed during the surveillance that Megan appeared to be flirting with Markoff, but he brushed her off. While one officer was busy calling Trisha, who had moved from Boston to New York City, to see if she could identify Markoff in a lineup at the station, the other officers watched Markoff and Megan, toting a small suitcase and knapsack, get into their car.

The police scrambled to keep an eye on Markoff as the car headed south on I-95. The couple was on their way to Foxwoods Casino in Connecticut. Meanwhile, police arranged for Trisha to meet a New York City detective to see if she could identify Markoff in a collection of photos. She did.

Police surrounded Markoff's car just south of Boston on I-95 and told him, "We have a warrant for this automobile and we need to take it back to Boston and you need to come with us."

During the ride to the police station, Megan asked Markoff several times what was going on, but he wouldn't respond. By the time they finally arrived at the Boston police station, she was frantic. The police put the couple into separate rooms, at which point Markoff asked for a lawyer. He was read his Miranda rights and told he was under arrest for kidnapping, armed robbery, and murder. Within minutes, he was booked and put into a holding cell. In a nearby room, Megan burst into tears when she learned her fiancé was under arrest.

For Trisha, it was good news. "As soon as they told me they had him in custody, I just started crying. I was very, very happy," she said. "It was like a weight had been lifted off my chest to know that he had finally been caught … and he can't hurt anybody else."

Everyone who knew Markoff and his family were shocked as details of his arrest hit the news media. Some of his friends set up a

Facebook group in his defense: Philip Markoff Is Innocent Until Proven Guilty.

Megan, who went to stay at her parents' house in New Jersey, couldn't believe Markoff had killed anyone, and defended him. "This is not the Philip Markoff that I know. … Philip is a beautiful man inside and out and would not hurt a fly."

But the evidence against Markoff kept mounting. Police found the gun used to kill Julissa in Markoff's apartment in a copy of *Gray's Anatomy*, a medical reference book that Markoff had hollowed out. During the investigation, police discovered that Markoff had used a fake ID to purchase the gun in New Hampshire in February 2009, which showed planning and premeditation on his behalf. Ballistic tests confirmed that his gun was the weapon used to kill Julissa.

Police found plastic zip ties similar to the ones used in the crimes, as well as several pairs of women's panties hidden in the apartment.

Then more stories about Markoff materialized. A former female friend of Markoff's recalled how Markoff once pushed her against the wall as he tried to kiss her in her apartment building.

"And I was saying, 'No, Phil," she said. "You know, we're just friends. What are you trying to do?'" She recalled that she tried to push him away. "And he was being forceful, and I physically couldn't get him off of me."

One of her friends arrived at the scene just in time to pull Markoff away from her. When he left the building, she shrugged off the incident, blaming the amount of alcohol they had both consumed earlier that evening. After Markoff was arrested, she wondered what might have happened if her friend hadn't come along that night.

A transvestite who had advertised on craigslist also contacted the police, claiming that he had exchanged emails with Markoff, who was using the screen name "sexaddict5385." Variations in that screen name led to other discoveries. "Sexaddict5385" was linked to a website called ALT.com for individuals interested in sexual encounters of an "adventurous" nature, including sadomasochism, bondage, and fetishes. The profile of "sexaddict5385" listed the use of chains, collars, leashes, and experimentation with transvestites among the user's interests. A photo of a man's naked torso was later confirmed by Boston police as Markoff's.

More than a few people were surprised to learn that Markoff was interested in acting as the submissive partner in a sadomasochistic homosexual tryst, given his track record as a heterosexual aggressor, but there was little doubt it was true. Related profiles were found on other websites, including gayclublist.com, passion.com, and extremerestraints.com. Although they couldn't be attributed directly to Markoff, the dates the accounts had been opened along with the supplied birthdates, screen names, and interests presented a consistent pattern.

In June 2009, a Boston grand jury indicted Markoff on first degree murder for Julissa's death and on the kidnapping and robbery of Trisha. He pled not guilty.

Markoff's fiancée visited him only two times while he was in jail; during her final visit, she said goodbye, telling him she had no idea that he had led a double life and couldn't believe she came so close to marrying a murderer.

On August 14, on what would have been their wedding day, Markoff carried out his carefully planned suicide. He had made a knife from a pen and piece of metal, according to Boston district attorney Dan Conley, then made a series of small wounds and deep cuts on his neck, arms, wrists, and ankles, using his medical knowledge to ensure his suicide was a success. His cuts included severing the femoral artery in one leg and the carotid artery in his neck. He wrapped a garbage bag over his leg to conceal the blood, and then put another bag over his head after stuffing paper towels down his throat to make it difficult to resuscitate him.

Over the jail cell door, Markoff had taken the time to write two words in his own blood: "Megan" and, just below that, "pocket"—a pet name they had for each other.

Markoff didn't leave a suicide note, which left some to speculate that he killed himself so Megan wouldn't have to testify at his trial. It seemed to many that he loved her, judging from the photos spread out all over his cell. Just as many believed he was being selfish, looking for the quickest way out.

The day after the suicide, Markoff's brother posted these words on his Facebook page: "Rest in peace, Phil. I will always love you."

Megan went on to medical school in the Caribbean, far from the media's eye but never far enough away from the haunting memories of a man she once loved who turned out to be the Craigslist Killer.

***

The Craigslist Killer didn't stop others from poring over the ads in the popular go-to site where people hope to connect with others or make a quick sale. For one family in Washington State, trying to sell a diamond ring cost them the life of one of their family members.

"Where's the safe? Where's the safe?" the young man screamed, waving a gun.

Confused, Jim Sanders stood and stared at the intruder in his Edgewater, Washington, home.

"I don't have one," Jim said, and the intruder began hitting and kicking him.

Just minutes before, at 9:00 PM on April 28, 2010, Jim had opened his front door and found a young couple on his front porch. The woman explained that she had called earlier about the heirloom diamond ring that Jim had advertised on craigslist. Jim hesitated for a moment, but the young man made sure that Jim could see that he had enough cash to pay for the ring on the spot. So Jim invited them into the house. The couple explained that they wanted to buy the ring as a Mother's Day gift and wanted to know more about it. Jim couldn't answer some of the questions, so he called his wife, Charlene Sanders, to join them in the kitchen.

As soon as Charlene was standing beside her husband, the young man pulled out a gun and told the couple to lie face down on the floor. His female accomplice tied their hands behind their backs with plastic ties.

Charlene and Jim told the intruders that their two sons, James Jr., 14, and Chandler, 10, were upstairs. But by this time two other men had made their way into the house, found the boys upstairs, and forced them at gunpoint into the kitchen. Both boys were ordered to lie face down on the floor next to their parents.

The men began kicking Charlene and told her to stop looking at them. One of them pointed a gun to her head, taunting her, "Three, two …"

Charlene remembers saying to herself, "Please, God, don't let them kill me in front of my kids." She began crying and said, "Just take what you want. Just don't kill us." But her pleas fell on deaf ears.

Days later, when a policeman stopped a car for a routine traffic violation in Daly City, California, a tale of murder began to unfold. The traffic stop turned out to be anything but routine: The police officer saw a bag of marijuana and a handgun on the car seat. The drugs and the gun were enough to arrest the driver and his two passengers—Kiyoshi Higashi, 22; Amanda Knight, 21; and Joshua Reese, 20—and hold them at the San Mateo (CA) County Jail for further questioning.

While the trio was being booked, a staff member at the San Mateo jail remembered hearing the news about a shooting in Washington State. Something about the threesome in the holding cells seemed to resonate with her. She talked to her boss, and her hunch turned out to be spot-on. But she didn't move fast enough. One of the suspects, Knight, had already posted bail and was headed back to Washington.

While the police were busy trying to trace Knight's whereabouts, she turned herself in to the Sumner Police Department in Washington just days later, on May 4. She didn't have much choice. Photos of her were plastered all over the television news and in the local papers; she had literally become the news of the day.

"You know who I am. You have the pictures of me," she said to the Sumner police, adding that she was "involved in the murder—the one in Edgewood." With that, police escorted her to an interrogation room and began questioning her. It wasn't long before Knight confessed on videotape to her involvement in the crime. When she had finished telling her side of the events, she put her head in her hands and sobbed.

She said it all started with an ad for an heirloom diamond ring that was posted on craigslist in the Puyallup/Edgewood, Washington, area on April 23, 2010. The stunning ring showcased a six-prong gold solitaire setting with brilliant-cut and baguette-cut diamonds totaling just over a caret and appraised at $2,760. The owner's home and cell phone numbers were listed underneath the ad. Little did Jim know that he had given these intruders a road map to his place. Jim had sold other items on craigslist before and never had any trouble. But this time, it was different.

The robbers had only one mission: to gather all the treasure they could find. But Jim wasn't helping. The first intruder was obviously agitated and hit Jim repeatedly in the head with a gun. James Jr. tried to protect his father, but the robber pistol-whipped him too, and he fell to the floor. While James Jr. was being attacked, the diversion gave Jim a chance to break the plastic ties around his wrists and jump on one of the robbers. During the scuffle, one of the other robbers shot Jim and dragged him out of the room.

The report from the Pierce County Sheriff's Department later noted that, "The suspects then drug … James from the kitchen to the living room where he was shot several more times."

During the shooting, Knight was busy going from room to room, stealing credit and debit cards, cell phones, iPods, ID cards, and, of course, the heirloom ring. She took Charlene's wedding band off her finger and kicked her in the head before the gang left the house.

Once the home invaders were gone, Charlene ran to her husband's side. "I just kept saying, 'Honey, please stay with me, stay with me, stay with us, don't go, don't go' and he was just barely gasping for air." At 9:28 PM, Chandler dialed 911 and told the operator, "My dad's been shot." But by then, Jim had died in his wife's arms.

The next day, the local police launched a search for the suspects, who they believed were tied to another craigslist ad robbery 60 miles away in Lake Stevens. The facts in the case were remarkably similar: The robbers tied the couple up, while two men stole a flat-screen TV that had been advertised on craigslist, as well as other electronic gear, money, and jewelry. The two men matched the descriptions that Charlene had provided of the men who terrorized her family along with the descriptions of the couple who had first entered the house.

The police conducted their initial search of the area and found several of the items that had been taken from the Sanderses' home near an off-ramp by a local highway.

Within the hour, Pierce County detectives arrived at the Sumner police station to question and pick up Knight. After the police talked to Knight, they apprehended Higashi and Reese, who were extradited to Washington State. The fourth suspect, Clabon Berniard, 23, turned himself in to the King County Jail in Seattle on May 6.

Derek Sanders, Jim's brother, was relieved that the suspects were apprehended so quickly. "We were worried that this might be something that went on for months and possibly years," he said. All four suspects were charged with first degree murder, two counts of robbery, and two counts of assault. Knight was sentenced to 71 years, Reese 100 years, Higashi 123 years, and Berniard 123 years.

While Higashi would eventually be charged with firing the shot that took Jim's life, at the time, Pierce County prosecuting attorney Mark Lindquist said it didn't matter who pulled the trigger; the four men would all face what he calls a "functional life sentence."

"It's really sad that there's so much evil," Charlene later told reporters. "I mean there's a lot of good in this world—and I've seen the good—but when I saw [Knight] I started to shake because I thought, 'Oh, they took my husband from me.'"

"You love your family," said Jim's father. "You can lose them in an instant. Just take them and hold them while you can and appreciate every moment you have with them. He always said he'd protect his family, he always told the boys he would protect his family, and he died protecting his family."

Jim and his family were so well-liked in the community that a local group generated $25,000 through a fundraiser to help the family.

An irony in this case is that one of the perpetrators, Berniard, had received the Citizen Lifesaving Award from the Skyway Fire Department for saving the lives of two elderly women 3 years earlier, having alerted the women to a house fire in 2007.

One of the women remembered Berniard and described him as a "very respectable, honorable young man" for his actions that day.

When she found out he was a suspect in the craigslist murder, she said she just couldn't believe it was the same man.

On May 10, Pierce County sheriff's detectives recovered the heirloom diamond ring that Jim had advertised on craigslist at a pawn shop in San Francisco.

"They took the love of my life, my future," said Charlene. "They ripped my home apart," all for a diamond ring.

Surveillance footage of Philip Markoff at the Westin Copley Place in Boston [Courtesy of Paul de la Rosa, Seven Days of Rage: The Deadly Crime Spree of the Craigslist Killer*]*

John Salsberg, Markoff's defense attorney [Courtesy of Paul de la Rosa, Seven Days of Rage: The Deadly Crime Spree of the Craigslist Killer*]*

Holiday Inn in Warwick, Rhode Island, where Markoff attacked his second victim [Courtesy of Paul de la Rosa, Seven Days of Rage: The Deadly Crime Spree of the Craigslist Killer*]*

Convicted killers of Jim Sanders, who attempted to sell jewelry through craigslist: [Top row, from left] Amanda Knight, Joshua Reese: [Bottom row, from left] Clabon Berniard, Kiyoshi Higashi [Courtesy of Pierce County Sheriff's Department]

About the Author

Breathless Focus Photography

Jayne A. Hitchcock is an internationally recognized cybercrime expert. She volunteers her time to work with the U.S. Department of Justice Office for Victims of Crime, the National Center for Victims of Crime, and numerous law enforcement agencies worldwide. As a valued resource to these agencies in solving internet-related crimes, she has also worked with legislators to draft and to pass many U.S. internet laws.

She also conducts law enforcement training seminars for local, county, state, military, and federal law enforcement agencies. Her speaking engagements on cybercrime and cyber safety include presentations at elementary, middle, and high schools, universities, and colleges. She also lectures at libraries, conferences, and corporations, while traveling extensively for presentations and workshops in the U.S., Canada, Europe, and at Sookmyung Women's University in Seoul, South Korea. She has been interviewed on several television shows including *America's Most Wanted*, *48 Hours*, *Primetime*, and *Good Morning America*, as well as local, national, and international newscasts, and in *Cosmopolitan* and *TIME* magazines. She was named a "Champion For Change" by Lifetime Television in 2004.

In addition to serving on the editorial board of the *International Journal of Cyber Crimes and Criminal Justice*, she writes for several magazines. She is also a member of Operations Security Professionals Society, Sisters in Crime, Inc. (national and New England divisions), National Rifle Association (lifetime member), the American Legion Ladies Auxiliary, and the Third Marine Division Association (lifetime member).

As president of two all-volunteer organizations, Working to Halt Online Abuse (WHOA) at www.haltabuse.org and the Kids/Teens Division (WHOA-KTD) at www.haltabusektd.org, Jayne continues her mission to educate adults and children about safety online. This is her 10th book; four are related to internet crime and six are about Okinawa and Iwo Jima, Japan.

More Great Books from Information Today, Inc.

Web of Deceit

Misinformation and Manipulation in the Age of Social Media

Edited by Anne P. Mintz

For all its amazing benefits, the worldwide social media phenomenon has provided manipulative people and organizations with the tools (and human targets) that allow hoaxes and con games to be perpetrated on a vast scale. In this eye-opening follow-up to her popular 2002 book, *Web of Deception*, Anne P. Mintz brings together a team of experts to explain how misinformation is intentionally spread and to illuminate the dangers in a range of critical areas. *Web of Deceit* is a must-read for any internet user who wants to avoid being victimized.

224 pp/softbound/ISBN 978-0-910965-91-0 $29.95

Net Crimes & Misdemeanors, 2nd Edition

Outmaneuvering Web Spammers, Stalkers, and Con Artists

By J. A. Hitchcock • Foreword by Vint Cerf

In this revised and expanded second edition of her popular book, cybercrime expert J. A. Hitchcock offers practical and easy-to-follow methods for dealing with spam, viruses, hack attacks, identity theft, and other online dangers. A lifeline for both individuals and business web users, the book covers a broad range of abusive practices and features dozens of firsthand anecdotes and success stories. A one-time victim of cyberstalking who fought back and won, Hitchcock went on to become a leading victim's advocate. Her readable and reassuring book is loaded with tips, strategies, and techniques as well as pointers to the laws, organizations, and web resources that can aid victims and help them fight back.

496 pp/softbound/ISBN 978-0-910965-72-9 $24.95